IMAGES OF GOD IN PRAYER

Rev. Joseph T. Muller, M.S.C., M.Ed.

To my beloved parents:

Joseph and Mary

Who now see Yahweh face to face

March, 2003
Aurora, Illinois

iii

ACKNOWLEDGEMENTS

This book began as a series of reflections on prayer which I intended to share with the Lay Associates of the Missionaries of the Sacred Heart. After reading them, a few of these friends encouraged me to pursue the idea of publication, so that the reflections might assist a wider audience.

I'm indebted to these friends, especially to Mr. Stephen Andras, who ultimately convinced me that I should make the effort to share these thoughts with a wider circulation. I also wish to thank Fr. Raymond Diesbourg, MSC, S.T.L., who offered valuable theological insights and who did the primary proofreading. Fr. Robert Cell, MSC, M.A., who did the thorough final proofreading, Fr. Ronald Leinen, MSC, Ph.D., who did the computer processing and who developed the index, Dr. Roy O'Neil, who offered invaluable professional editorial advice, and Jody Watermann, who did the final editing, all merit my sincerest gratitude.

If this small volume helps to make a difference in the prayer life of only one person, it has been worth the effort.

FOREWORD

Every so often a frank and refreshing volume on prayer appears that promises to be a genuine help in fostering union with God. This is one of those books.

The author shares candidly how others affected him in his own on-and-off search for intimacy with God. He then moves into the body of his work: the importance of images of God to prayer life. By highlighting this imagery in the whole of Scripture, he makes his point. By showing how the great prayers of the Catholic Church also assume this viewpoint, he reinforces his message. His concluding observations on perseverance in prayer are well worth heeding.

I find the most valuable point of the book to lie in the author's ability to make the reader aware of his own latent desire to know God intimately, a desire that never completely fades, nor is completely sated, until his Maker enables him to see Him face-to-face.

The author believes that those who face up to this desire are the ones who will achieve the greatest measure of happiness allotted to human beings in this world. He believes that those who ignore it will find themselves inexplicably restless, no matter how successful they appear to be.

Facing up to the desire involves a decision to assign a block of daily life solely for the purpose of listening to God and allowing Him to reveal himself.

Apparently, this classic, time-proven method has proven successful for the author. I believe his enthusiasm will infect readers and entice them to try it out as well. As the author points out in his conclusion:

"All the saints and all spiritual writers of merit...know that God is always revealing himself. So they work at perfecting their ability to listen through prayer. And the more they listen, the more they receive. The more they receive, the more fascinated they become. The more fascinated they become, the more they want to listen and receive. The more they receive, the more they want to share. The more they share, the more they receive."

Stephen J. Andras
Cogan Productions

TABLE OF CONTENTS

"Yahweh, I seek your face" (Ps 27:8).

PREFACE

The older I get the more I am convinced that God has placed in every human being a desire to know him intimately. The fact that most people don't understand this desire, or consciously think about it, or do things to keep it from surfacing, does not diminish its reality. Like a dimly glowing ember, this desire lies there waiting to be fanned into a roaring flame. As the great St. Augustine once wrote: "You made us for yourself and our hearts are restless, till they rest in You" (*The Confessions of St. Augustine* Book One, I).

Only those who have become familiar with the true God can effectively fan the flame in others. In reflecting on my experience, I'm amazed at how many of these people there are in the world. I'm also intrigued at how ordinary and unspectacular most of them are.

In truth, I'm one of these ordinary, unspectacular people, yet for years I've had a desire to share how God has gradually and patiently brought me to an understanding of who He really is. In particular, I've had a desire to share how He accomplished this through a number of very common people, through experiences and insights that have come my way, especially as I read the Sacred Scriptures.

These Scriptures tell us that God has made us in His own image (Gn 1:27), but what does that mysterious sentence mean, since the same Scriptures tell us that God is spirit and not flesh? (Jn 4:24). Scriptural scholars tell us that the sentence in Genesis means that God has given our spirit the power to know and to choose, to fashion things and to love, to live forever. However, is it just possible that all the wholesome images we have of ourselves and of nature are somehow contained in God and are capable of revealing something of his very being to us? If "in him we live and move and have our being" (Acts 17:28), then somehow this must be true. In fact, God has chosen to reveal himself to us through these created images.

Images do more than convey ideas; they convey feelings about ideas as well. And when we begin to pray it is important to realize this. For prayer is not merely an intellectual exercise, but a total response of our being to God. How we see God has definite emotional overtones. He has chosen to reveal himself in a variety of images that captivate our imaginations, impelling us to goodness, or dissuading us from evil until we see him face to face in eternity.

Although I am far from any complete understanding of the wonderful being we call God, I feel impelled to put my thoughts on paper, to share how God has aided my search to know him. Hopefully, my words will stimulate you who read them to reflect prayerfully on your experiences and on God's words, and in so doing develop a deep personal relationship with him.

So I write, compelled by the Spirit of Goodness to encourage you who are conscious of your restlessness. Open yourself to God as he reveals himself in the Scriptures, in nature, and in the experiences of your life. I write, like John, to make my own joy complete (1 Jn 1:4).

CHAPTER ONE

CHRIST, OUR GOD MADE VISIBLE

In his first letter to Timothy, Paul wrote these striking words: "Without any doubt, the mystery of our religion is very deep indeed: God was made visible in the flesh, attested by the Spirit, seen by angels, proclaimed to the pagans, believed in by the world, taken up in glory" *(1 Tm 3:16)*. The writer of Hebrews, who knew of the ascension of Christ, goes on to say: "Let us not lose sight of Jesus, who leads us in our faith and brings it to perfection: for the sake of the joy which was still in the future, he endured the cross, disregarding the shamefulness of it and from now on has taken his place at the right of God's throne. Think of the way he stood such opposition from sinners and then you will not give up for want of courage" *(Heb 12:2-4)*.

Thoughtful people instinctively know that there is a power higher than themselves, a power from whom they have come, a power responsible for this planet, for the universe itself. They wonder about who it might be. They speculate and evolve theodicies based on reason and theologies based on revelations. They want to know this power, even though they are awed by the myriads of creations, their grandeur and complexities. They yearn to see and to hear this awesome being whom they call God in ten thousand different tongues. Why? Instinctively they sense that he is good, that he is interested in their welfare, that he can help them live healthier, happier, more peaceful lives. Sane persons are not attracted to someone who is evil, who hates them and wants to bring them sickness, misery and strife.

No one knows the origins of every religion. However, the desire to make contact with God underlies them all, burning more fiercely in some individuals than in others. Some have reached out to God in ritual actions, prayers and chants. Some of them claimed to have been contacted by God, or by one of his agents through visions or dreams.

1

Some claimed to have received messages of great importance for the welfare of the people around them. People who believe their words, who enter into their rituals and use their prayers, hope their lives will become better through their worship.

In this regard, the Hebrews were no different from the many primitive tribes of Papua New Guinea, with whom I worked for twenty-four years. They wanted to know the power, or powers, which ruled their bodies, and all the forces of nature. They sensed that their lives would be better if they succeeded. Life was short and difficult; troubles and enemies were many. They felt alone and afraid. They hoped it didn't have to stay this way. They hoped that God would give them answers, remove their fears, and make their lives more meaningful.

Jews, Christians and Moslems alike believe that God selected one of the Hebrews, a man called Abram, for a special revelation. In it God promised to bless (make happy) all the peoples of the earth through a descendant of Abram. God's choice made it clear that his unconditional love was the source of the blessing rather than Abram's renown or talents. Abram was an unknown desert nomad whom God commanded to leave his familiar surroundings, to live as a stranger in a foreign land. Although Abram and his wife Sara were well past the age of having children, they were promised a son. Several more years passed before they realized Isaac's joyous birth. Then God asked Abram to sacrifice this beloved child. Through all these tests Abram believed what God had spoken. As a reward, God reaffirmed his promise and changed his name to Abraham (Father of many nations). God repeated this great promise to Isaac and to his son, Jacob, later extending it to Judah and David's lineage as well.

Paul, in his letter to the Romans, pointed out that God selected Abraham to show that deliverance and reconciliation with God and with one another comes from faith in the power of God, rather than from reliance on human philosophy. Faith also shows that God achieved this in a way no human being could even imagine. Deliverance and reconciliation would indeed take place through a descendant of David. But the descendant would be God himself, who chose to be born of a virgin espoused to a man called Joseph of the house of David (*Lk 1:26 ff.*). The four Gospels are unique in the Scriptures, for they alone offer us portrayals of the Son of God.

Matthew begins his Gospel with the genealogy of Jesus, Son of God, Son of Joseph and Mary, to demonstrate the fulfillment of God's promise to Abraham. Scholars tell us that a major portion of his Gospel is a verbal portrayal of Jesus as the new Moses who teaches his people what they must do to be saved, to achieve the good things that his Father has prepared for those who love him.

Luke also includes a genealogy (*Lk 3:23-38*), but he begins with the human opinion about Jesus and leads his readers to accept the faith God wants them to have in Jesus, as the "son of God" -- a God who loves all people and wants them to be saved. The verbal picture which Luke paints of Jesus is that of a person concerned about the plight of ordinary people, of women, of outcasts, of those who feel unloved, unvalued, lost and forgotten.

Mark, on the other hand, offers no genealogy because his principal interest is to present Jesus as the Power of God made flesh for our benefit. John gives no genealogy either, but begins his Gospel by going to the very heart of the matter: our human desire to know God, to see him, to be guided, protected and blessed by him. We can never fully appreciate the grandeur of his words: "He (Jesus) was with God in the beginning. Through him all things came to be, not one thing had its being but through him... He lived among us, and we saw his glory... No one has ever seen God; it is the only Son, who is nearest to the Father's heart, who has made him known" (*Jn 1:1-18*).

In her liturgy the church has with good reason a daily reading from the Gospels. These readings bring us face to face with the God who loves us so much that he became one like us. Why did he do something so remarkable? Couldn't he have taught us the same lessons and worked the same miracles through another human being

3

to reveal God's love and concern for us? Even if he could, our yearning to know our God would still remain. The need of atonement for sin, which Christ accomplished, would still remain. The desire to know what happens after death would still gnaw at our minds. We would still lack the internal strength of spirit to believe and to follow faithfully the teachings and admonitions of our loving God.

Each Gospel reveals through Jesus the tenderness of our God. No matter how many times we revisit the stories of Matthew, Mark, Luke and John we are touched by Jesus' teaching, concern, and power: power over nature and sickness and sin. Yet he seems greatest in his forgiveness of enemies, in his suffering and death borne in our name, for our sins--and of course, in his glorious resurrection from the dead.

Private prayer, like the liturgy, needs to be centered on getting to know Jesus, for Jesus is our God made visible. Jesus is a human being, like us. He experienced all our needs, passions, hopes, fears and desires. Jesus lived in a family, which dwelt in a small town, in a small country dominated by foreign powers. He learned from his parents, relatives, friends and teachers. Jesus worked with his hands to earn his bread. From an ordinary boy he grew into a man, until his Father's appointed time had come. Then Jesus began to teach in his own name and with power that was unmistakably divine.

With Jesus as our friend and guide, we can revisit the other Scriptures that speak about him and of his triumph over the evils brought on by sin. We can better understand the cry of the human family for help. We can appreciate the longing of people to see their great Creator who takes such interest in them. We can better appreciate the light which God has shed upon himself and upon the great mysteries of creation, life, good and evil, suffering, death and life hereafter.

CHAPTER TWO

IMAGES OF GOD IN THE PSALMS

Outside of the Gospels, no single book in Scripture has given us a clearer view of God than the book of Psalms. Accordingly, the book of Psalms has remained the principal prayer book of God's people in both Old and New Testaments. Jesus and his apostles frequently used these sacred songs. Every Mass contains at least one of the Psalms, which also form the heart of the breviary. Saints, Popes, Doctors and Fathers of the church frequently quoted the Psalms, making them the basis of their meditations. The Psalms span the entire Old Testament and encapsulate the yearning of the human heart for intimacy with God. They express our human yearning to be free of the evils brought on by sin. They acknowledge personal guilt, cry out to God for help and sing praises for his assistance.

The language of the Psalms is earthy and appeals to the imagination. The authors, many over a long period of time, picture God in many different ways. These pictures, inspired by God himself, give us a glimpse of who he really is: pure goodness, power, mercy and love.

The pictures, incomplete as each may be, help us to understand something of our wonderful, loving God and of the Son he sent to save us.

Almost every Psalm presents us with some image on which to focus. It seems that God knows how prone we are to distractions and so gives us something visual to grasp as we turn to him in prayer. I've tried to group together the Psalms which contain similar images. The grouping is not definitive, because some Psalms contain more than one image. I hope that readers will be stimulated to meditate upon these sacred songs and so grow to appreciate these glimpses of God and his Son, Jesus, which are hidden in them.

5

NATURAL IMAGES OF GOD IN THE PSALMS

Three images, all drawn from nature, recur in several psalms: *water*, as illustrated in streams and rain, *birds* which appear as hens and eagles, and *mountains*, in the form of rocks, cliffs and other high places. Like water, God gives life and refreshes. Like a bird, he vigorously protects his own and like a mountain, he offers safety from enemies.

We find water images in general Psalms:
- "Happy the man who...finds his pleasure in the law of Yahweh...he is like a tree that is planted by water streams, yielding its fruit in due season..." *(Ps 1:1-3)*.
- "As the doe longs for running streams, so my soul for you, my God" *(Ps 42:1)*.
- "My soul is thirsting for you, my flesh is longing for you, as a land parched, weary and waterless" *(Ps 63:1)*.
- "You visit the earth and water it, you load it with riches" *(Ps 65:8)*.
- "Like thirsty ground I yearn for you" *(Ps 143:6)*.

Bird imagery, also appears in various Psalms:
- "Hide me in the shadow of your wings from the onslaughts of the wicked" *(Ps 17:8)*.
- "The sons of men take shelter in the shadow of your wings" *(Ps 36:7)*.
- "I take shelter in the shadow of your wings, until the destroying storm is over" *(Ps 57:1)*.
- "Let me stay in your tent forever, taking refuge in the shelter of your wings" *(Ps 61:4)*.
- "I sing for joy in the shadow of your wings" *(Ps 63:7)*.
- "He covers you with his feathers and you shall find shelter underneath his wings" *(Ps 91:4)*.

We also find in the Psalms various images of the mountains:
- "Yahweh is my rock and my bastion" *(Ps 18:2)*.
- "Yahweh...my rock...a saving fortress for his anointed" *(Ps 28)*.
- "Your favor, Yahweh, stood me on a peak impregnable" *(Ps 30:7)*.
- "Lead me to your holy mountain" *(Ps 43:3)*.
- "To the rock too high for me, lead me" *(Ps 61:2)*.
- "With him along for my rock, my safety, my fortress, I can never fall" *(Ps 62:2)*.
- "Be a sheltering rock for me, a walled fortress to save me" *(Ps 71:3)*.
- "Come let us praise...the Rock of our safety" *(Ps 95:1)*.
- "Jerusalem! Encircled by mountains, as Yahweh encircles his people" *(Ps 125:2)*.
- "Blessed be Yahweh, my rock...my savior" *(Ps 144:1-2)*.

THE PSALMS' IMAGES OF GOD
DRAWN FROM HUMAN RELATIONS

Most of the images of the Psalms, however, are drawn from human relations. These fall into two major groupings: those stressing the power of God and others emphasizing his concern and affection for human beings.

The following Psalms offer us human images which convey God's power:
- Yahweh, the King: *Psalms 2, 5, 21, 24, 45, 47, 93, 95, 97, 99, 101, 110, 112, 113, 132, 145, 149.*
- Yahweh, Creator and Master of the World: *Psalms 8, 19, 29, 50, 83, 95, 96, 100, 104, 114, 115, 121, 148, 149.*
- Yahweh, the Just Judge: *Psalms 9, 10, 17, 26, 58, 67, 75, 82, 94, 98, 99, 111, 129, 146.*
- Yahweh, the Great Desert Chieftain: *Psalms 15, 52, 76.*

- Yahweh, the Champion Warrior: *Psalms 22, 35, 44, 59, 64, 108, 124.*
- Yahweh, the Wonder-worker: *Psalms 78, 105, 135, 136, 150.*

Our faith finds strength reinforced in theses images of the power of God.

Human images that convey the concern and affection of God are found in these Psalms:
- Yahweh, the Guardian: *Psalms 3, 4, 7, 68, 72, 74.*
- Yahweh, the Savior: *Psalms 7, 20, 32, 38, 39, 40, 54, 55, 56, 60, 69, 70, 81, 85, 86, 88, 91, 97, 102, 103, 107, 109, 111, 116, 118, 120, 123, 126, 130, 138, 140, 141, 142, 143.*
- Yahweh, the Watchful Overseer: *Psalms 11, 53.*
- Yahweh, the Lover: *Psalms 13, 33, 117.*
- Yahweh, the Wise Teacher: *Psalms 14, 16, 25, 49, 73, 90, 139.*
- Yahweh, the Good Shepherd: *Psalms 23, 77, 79, 80, 95, 100, 119.*
- Yahweh, the Concerned Physician: *Psalms 30, 41, 103, 147.*
- Yahweh, the Faithful Provider: *Psalms 34, 36, 37, 111.*
- Yahweh, the Peacemaker: *Psalm 46.*
- Yahweh, the Purifier: *Psalms 51, 66.*
- Yahweh, the Loving Father: *Psalms 89, 103, 133.*
- Yahweh, the Careful Gardener: *Psalm 92.*
- Yahweh, the Wise Law-giver: *Psalms 119, 128, 147.*

From these Psalms' imagery of God's love and affection, our position as his loving children is reinforced.

IMAGES OF GOD IN THE PSALMS
DRAWN FROM MAN-MADE OBJECTS

The history of the Hebrews deals inextricably with fighting for survival. In those times shields and stone walls (fortress) offered protection from human enemies, just as tents offered them relief from sun and storms. Oil lamps provided light needed to see the enemy and to overcome fear. Quite naturally, the sacred writers would look upon God as their shield, their solid wall behind whom they found safety, their sheltering tent, and as a light in battle. But Jerusalem, the Holy City, also fired the imaginations of those inspired writers, especially after Solomon's construction of the magnificent temple. They saw Yahweh in the beauty, order and peace of the Holy City. They longed to dwell here, where all was lovely and where the people all lived in friendship and tranquility.

- Yahweh, the Shield is found in the following Psalms: Psalms 3, 5, 7, 18, 33, 34, 35, 84, 90, 91, 115, 144.
- Images of Yahweh, the Wall or Fortress is found in general Psalms as well: *Psalms 9, 18, 27, 28, 31, 48, 59, 62, 71, 84, 91, 94, 144.*
- Yahweh, the Tent is found in *Psalms 15, 27, 34, 43, 55.*
- Yahweh, the Lamp appears in *Psalm 18.*
- And finally, Yahweh, the Holy City is demonstrated in *Psalms 48, 87, 122, 134, 137.*

CHAPTER THREE

IMAGES OF GOD IN THE PROPHETS

As the psalmist presents God in his favorite image of inspiration, so do the prophets and other writers of both Testaments. Each of these inspired images of God helps us understand something of our Creator. God, like pure light, can't be seen. He must pass through the prisms of our individual experiences. Here He appears as the gold of a majestic ruler, the red of a compassionate friend, the blue of a faithful spouse, the green of a caring parent, the purple of a forgiving father, the brown of a concerned shepherd, the yellow of a wise teacher. Each color is hidden in the pure light, but none embodies wholly the pure light. Each image tells us something about God, but none completely captures His identity. Yet we need these images to help us pray until God enables us to see Him face to face.

FIRST ISAIAH (Chapters 1-39)

Scholars believe that the Book of Isaiah contains three distinct accounts by different authors.

First Isaiah lived in a time of turmoil. His mission from Yahweh was to announce the fall of the kingdoms of Israel and Judah, as punishment for their injustice. But he was also to announce the promise of survival for those who would repent. Under divine inspiration, Isaiah used strong imagery of Yahweh, images that foster our faith and understanding of God.

God the Concerned Father

Isaiah pictures Yahweh speaking to all of creation about his disappointment over the rebelliousness of his children: "Listen, you heavens; earth attend, for Yahweh is speaking: 'I reared sons, I brought them up, but they have rebelled against me. The ox knows its

10

owner and the ass its master's crib; Israel knows nothing, my people understands nothing. A sinful nation, a people weighed down with guilt, a breed of wrongdoers, perverted sons' " *(Is 1:2-4)*.

God the Teacher

God then goes on to give his perverted sons some instruction that they might avoid the awful consequences of their sins: "Cease to do evil. Learn to do good. Search for justice. Help the oppressed. Be just to the orphan. Plead for the widow" *(Is 1:16-17)*. "He who acts with integrity, who speaks sincerely and rejects extortionate profit, who waves away bribes from his hands, shuts suggestions of murder out of his ears and closes his eyes against crime; this man will dwell in the heights, he will find refuge in a citadel built on rock" *(Is 33:15-16)*. Worship without conversion of heart stupefies the mind and blinds the eye *(Is 29:9-14)*.

God the Bleacher

Isaiah writes that if Israel repents, then God promises to wash away their sins. "Though your sins are like scarlet, they shall be as white as snow, though they are red as crimson, they shall be like wool" *(Is 1:18)*.

God the Just Judge

God will not be mocked. Israel will reap what she sows. "If you are willing to obey, you shall eat the good things of the earth. But if you persist in rebellion, the sword shall eat you instead. The mouth of Yahweh has spoken" *(Is 1:19-20)*.

God the Master Silversmith

As a smith removes impurities in the fire, so God intends to remove injustice from his people, by plunging them into the crucible of suffering: "I will turn my hand against you. I will smelt away your

11

dross in the furnace. I will remove all your base metal from you...then you will be called City of Integrity, Faithful City. Zion will be redeemed by justice and her penitents by integrity" *(Is 1:25-27)*.

God the Peacemaker

It is God's will that all nations of the earth find Yahweh through Israel and in finding him turn away from ways of injustice and oppression: "He will wield authority over the nations and adjudicate between many people; these will hammer their swords into plowshares, their spears into sickles. Nation will not lift sword against nation, there will be no more training for war" *(Is 2:4-5)*. Isaiah pictures God actively creating peace, in the world and in our hearts.

God the King of Kings

Those who trust in their own magic, wealth, chariots, ships, or pride will be brought low. God will allow their enemies to despoil and enslave them, so that the survivors will remember who rules this earth, and also the holiness he demands. "Your men will fall by the sword, your heroes in the fight ... those who are left of Zion and remain of Jerusalem shall be called holy and those left in Jerusalem, noted down for survival" *(Is 3:25-26 and 4:1-3)*.

God the Tent of Shelter

The humble will seek refuge in Yahweh and he will not deny it to them. "The glory of Yahweh will be a canopy and a tent to give shade by day from the heat, refuge and shelter from the storm and rain *(Is 4:6)*.

God the Vine Grower

God cares for his people like a concerned vine grower. He expects the sweet, abundant fruit of justice from them, but if they instead produce the sour grapes of injustice, he will abandon his vineyard temporarily to the briars of barbarians, as in *Is 5:5*. However, God will reclaim the humbled after a period of time as in *Is 27:2-3*.

God the Physician

God has determined that radical surgery is necessary in order to save the body of Israel. He wants all his people to turn from injustice and thus be healed. Since most of them will not repent, however, many will therefore die, only a tenth of the people remaining *(Is 6)*. Yet Yahweh longs to heal those who return to him. "Then Yahweh will dress the wound of his people and heal the bruises his blows have left" *(Is 30:26)*.

God the Champion Warrior

If God's people remain loyal to him, he will overcome their enemies; if not, they will be enslaved. Weapons and political pacts will not save them; only conversion to God will do that. "If you do not stand by me, you will not stand at all" *(Is 7:9b)*. "They make alliances not inspired by me and so add sin to sin" *(Is 30:1)*.

God the Prince of Peace

As fear and despair begin to overwhelm the people, God renews his promise to send a ruler from the line of David who will save them from the oppression of sin. Christians see in Jesus this promised savior. With countless others we thrill to the majestic poetry of Isaiah: "For the yoke that was weighing on him, the bar across his shoulders, the rod of his oppressor, these you break as on the day of Midian. For all the foot gear of battle, every cloak rolled in blood, is burned and consumed by fire. For there is a child born for us, a son given to us and dominion is laid on his shoulders. And this is the name they give him: Wondrous Counselor, Mighty God, Eternal Father, Prince of Peace. Wide is his dominion in a peace that has no end, for the throne of David and for his royal power, which he

13

establishes and makes secure in justice and integrity. From this time onward and forever, the jealous love of Yahweh Sabaoth will do this" *(Is 9:3-7)*.

This message reappears in chapter eleven: "A shoot springs from the stock of Jesse (David's father) a scion thrusts from his roots: on him the spirit of Yahweh rests, a spirit of wisdom and insight, a spirit of counsel and power, a spirit of knowledge and fear of Yahweh ... Integrity is the loincloth round his waist, faithfulness the belt about his hips. The wolf lives with the lamb, the panther lies down with the kid, calf and lion cub feed together with a little boy to lead them. The cow and the bear make friends, their young lie down together. The lion eats straw like the ox. The infant plays over the cobra's hole; into the viper's lair the young child puts his hand. They do no hurt, no harm, on all my holy mountain, for the country is filled with the knowledge of Yahweh as the waters swell the sea" *(Is 11:1-9)*.

God the Absolute Ruler

God uses the barbarians to discipline the people of Israel. They, in turn, will be humbled to check their arrogance: "When the Lord has completed all his work on Mount Zion and in Jerusalem, he will punish what comes from the king of Assyria's boastful heart and his arrogant insolence ... Yahweh is going to send a wasting sickness on his stout warriors ... on that day the survivors of the House of Jacob will truly rely on Yahweh ..." *(Is 10:12,16, 20* and also in chapters *30, 31, 33, 34, 37)*. This punishment will be extended to the Chaldeans as well. Chapter thirteen depicts the awful scene of retribution by the Medes, while chapter twenty-one reviews this horror. Chapter fourteen lampoons the empty glory of the king of Babylon by the spirits of the dead: "You, too, have become like us. Your magnificence has been flung down ... underneath you a bed of maggots and over you a blanket of worms ..." *(Is 14:10-11)*. The Philistines and Moabites as well as those in Damascus will also wail as their lands are stripped and their people driven into the wilderness (Is 14-17). Also the king of Assyria will be Yahweh's rod of

14

punishment on Ethiopia and Egypt *(Is 18, 19, 20, 31)*.

The desert tribes of Edom, Dedan, Kedar will also feel the heel of the tyrant *(Is 20, 21)*. The maritime nations of Tyre and Sidon will also be devastated *(Is 23)*. Evil will consume the inhabitants of the earth, until they acknowledge their accountability to Yahweh. "The earth is defiled under its inhabitants' feet, for they have transgressed the law, violated the precept, broken the everlasting covenant. So a curse consumes the earth and its inhabitants suffer the penalty..." *(Is 24:5)*.

God the Water of Life

Isaiah speaks of "the converted" — those who accept the God of Jacob as their own. The converted will come to realize that God did not reject his people; they rejected him and through sin dug only dry wells. That some were saved is a sign of God's great mercy. These will sing: "I have trust now and no fear, for Yahweh is my strength, my song, he is my salvation. You will draw water joyfully from the springs of salvation" *(Is 12:2-3)*.

God the Generous Host

The converted will enjoy an abundance of good things; they will sing and rejoice in God's goodness: "Yahweh will prepare for all people a banquet of rich food, a banquet of fine wines ... he will remove the mourning veil ... he will destroy death forever. Yahweh will wipe away the tears from every cheek; he will take away his people's shame ... We exult and rejoice that he has saved us ..."
(Is 25:6-9).

God the Citadel Built on Rock

The converted will find safety in Yahweh. They will sing: "We have a strong city; to guard us he has set wall and rampart about us. Open the gates! Let the upright come in ... Trust in Yahweh forever, for Yahweh is the everlasting Rock ..." *(Is 26:1-4)*.

God the Stonemason

With the converted, God will erect a new house. The cornerstone of the building will be justice and holiness. The future ruler will be eminently a man concerned with these virtues. "See how I lay in Zion a stone of witness, a precious cornerstone, a foundation stone. The believer shall not stumble. And I will make justice the measure, integrity the plumb line" *(Is 28:16-17)*.

God the Understanding Farmer

Yahweh will break hardened hearts with the plow and harrow of suffering, but only to plant the wheat and barley of understanding and virtue. He flails and drags the grains, not to crush them, but to release them from the hulls of sin *(Is 28)*.

God the Potter

God made us and understands us through and through as a potter does the work of his hands. To reject this fact, to attempt to live with no accountability to God is foolish. It's as if the pot could say to the potter: "You didn't make me" or "I think your ways of doing things are foolish." Wisdom will only be attained when people admit their dependency on God and their accountability to him *(Is 29)*.

AMOS

The weather-beaten shepherd Amos, like First Isaiah, felt impelled by God to call the Israelites to repentance. His imagery, as we might expect, is pastoral, but frank and blunt. Still the language of Amos retains an enduring power, furthering our understanding of God.

16

God the Just Judge

The inhabitants of Israel and her neighbors will be punished because of their hard-heartedness and repeated injustices: "Yahweh says ... I will not relent ... because they have sold the virtuous man for silver and the poor man for a pair of sandals, because they trample on the heads of ordinary people and push the poor out of their path, because father and son have both resorted to the same girl, profaning my holy name, because they stretch themselves out by the side of every altar on clothes acquired as pledges and drink the wine of the people they have fined in the house of their god ..." *(Am 2:6-8)*.

God the Teacher

Amos shows us that life and death are chosen states of being. God encourages us to choose ways of acting that promote life. "Seek good and not evil, so that you may live, and that Yahweh may really be with you as you claim he is. Hate evil, love good, maintain justice ... that Yahweh may take pity on the remnant of Joseph" *(Am 5:14-15)*.

Avoid formalism in religion. It fosters a feeling of self-righteousness without promoting a change of heart. "I reject your oblations and refuse to look at your sacrifices of fattened cattle. Let me have no more of the din of your chanting, no more of your strumming on harps. But let justice flow like water and integrity like an unfailing stream" *(Am 5:22-24)*.

God the Savior

The enemies of Israel appear as consuming as locusts and as devastating as drought, but a remnant of the people will be saved. "Yet I am not going to destroy the House of Jacob completely ... I will re-erect the tottering hut of David ..." *(Am 9:9-11)*.

HOSEA

With the fall of the Northern Kingdom of Israel imminent, Yahweh sent yet another prophet to call his people to a change of heart. Hosea's painful experiences caused by his unfaithful wife, Gomer, moved him to write in yet a different vein about Yahweh.

God the Forgiving Husband

God has joined himself to his people, as a man with a wife. He has lavished his care and affection on them. Yet they forget his gifts and give their attention and affection to those who despise them. Despite repeated infidelities, God cannot bring himself to reject them. He continues to lavish his gifts upon them, because he loves them. "I was the one who was giving her the corn, the wine, the oil ... silver and gold" *(Hos 2:8)*. "I am going to lure her and lead her out into the wilderness and speak to her heart. I am going to give her back her vineyards. There she will respond to me as she did when she was young as she did when she came out of the land of Egypt" *(Hos 2:14-15)*.

God the Just Judge

The majority of the people, however, seem unwilling to change. They love their sinful excesses and think they can avoid punishment by military might and clever political pacts. But they are mistaken. "Israel has forgotten his Maker and has built palaces. Judah has built fortified town after fortified town. Right, I will rain fire on his towns, it will devour his palaces" *(Hos 8:14)*. Also, exile in Egypt and Assyria await the unfaithful. "Because they have not listened to him, my God will cast them off and they will be wanderers throughout the nations" *(Hos 9:17)*. "They will have to go back to Egypt, Assyria must be their king, because they have refused to return to me" *(Hos 11:5)*.

18

JEREMIAH

The kingdom of Israel had disappeared, its ten tribes deported to Assyria. Now the Chaldeans threatened to inflict the same fate on the kingdom of Judah. Impelled by the spirit of Yahweh, Jeremiah, a man who loved peace, is sent to prophesy disaster and punishment to a people who hated his message and refused to change their ways. The mission revolted Jeremiah, but he carried it out faithfully. Personal rejection, persecution, suffering, exile and finally death were his rewards. Only later were his greatness and wisdom appreciated by the people of God. Jeremiah's intimacy with God was unrivaled. The images he used to enlighten and move his stubborn countrymen still captivate and stir the soul.

God Creator and Supreme Ruler

"Will you not tremble at my presence, I who set the sands as limit to the sea ... who gives the rain ... who assures weeks appointed for harvest ..." *(Jer 5:22, 24)*.

God the Forgiving Husband

"I remember the affection of your youth, the love of your bridal days. You followed me through the wilderness ... what shortcoming did your fathers find in me that led them to desert me? I brought you to a fertile country to enjoy its produce and good things, but no sooner had you entered than you defiled my land ... they have abandoned me, the fountain of living water only to dig cisterns for themselves, leaky cisterns that hold no water ... does a girl forget her ornaments, a bride her sash? And yet my people have forgotten me, for days beyond number" *(Jer 2:1-32)*. "You maintained a prostitute's bold front, never thinking to blush ... you, the friend of my youth ... you were so obstinate" *(Jer 3:3-5)*.

"Come back, disloyal Israel — it is Yahweh who speaks — since I am merciful ... I shall not keep my resentment forever. Only

19

acknowledge your guilt ..." *(Jer 3:12-13)*. "If you wish to come back, Israel — it is Yahweh who speaks — it is to me you must return ... If you swear, 'As Yahweh lives!', truthfully, justly, honestly, the nations will bless themselves by you ..." *(Jer 4:1-2)*.

"I am in anguish ... my heart is throbbing ... for I have heard the trumpet call and the cry of war ... the whole land is laid waste ... this is because my people are stupid, they do not know me ... they are clever enough at doing wrong, but do not know how to do right ... you may dress yourself in scarlet, put on ornaments of gold, enlarge your eyes with paint but you make yourself pretty in vain. Your lovers disdain you; your life is what they are seeking ..." *(Jer 4:19, 22, 30)*. "A nation whose tongue you do not know ... will devour your harvest and food, devour your sons and daughters, devour your flocks and herds, devour your vines and fig trees, bring down your fortified towns in which you put your trust. Yet even in those days--it is Yahweh who speaks--I shall not completely destroy you" *(Jer 5:15-18)*.

God the Teacher

"Yahweh says this: Put yourselves on the ways of long ago. Inquire about the ancient paths. Which was the good way? Take it then and you shall find rest" *(Jer 6:16)*. Formal worship without conversion is unacceptable. "What do I care about incense imported from Sheba, or fragrant cane from a distant country? Your holocausts are not acceptable, your sacrifices do not please me" *(Jer 6:20)*. "Amend your behavior and I will stay with you here in this place. Put no trust in delusive words like these: This is the sanctuary of Yahweh, the sanctuary of Yahweh, the sanctuary of Yahweh! But if you treat each other fairly, if you do not exploit the stranger, the orphan and the widow ... then I will stay with you, in the land that long ago I gave to your father forever" *(Jer 7:3-7)*. "When I brought your ancestors out of the land of Egypt, I said nothing to them, gave them no orders about burnt offerings and sacrifice. These were my orders: Listen to my voice, then I will be your God and you shall be my people.

20

Follow right to the end the way that I mark out for you and you will prosper" *(Jer 7:22-24)*.

God the Potter

"As the clay is in the potter's hand, so you are in mine. On occasion, I decree for some nation, for some kingdom, that I will tear up, knock down, destroy; but if this nation, against which I have pronounced sentence, abandons its wickedness, I then change my mind about the evil which I had intended to inflict on it. On another occasion, I decree for some nation, for some kingdom, that I will build up and plant; but if that nation does what displeases me, refusing to listen to my voice, I then change my mind about the good which I had intended to confer on it" *(Jer 18:6-11)*.

God the Physician

"Your wound is incurable, your injury past healing. There is no one to care for your sore, no medicine to make you well again ... but I will restore you to health and heal your wounds. It is Yahweh who speaks" *(Jer 30:12,17)*. "I will hasten their recovery and their cure; I will cure them and let them know peace and security in full measure" *(Jer 33:6)*.

God the Loving Father

"I have loved you with an everlasting love, so I am constant in my affection for you ... for I am a father to Israel and Ephraim is my first-born son ..." *(Jer 31:3,9)*.

God the Gardener

"Deep within them I will plant my Law, writing it on their hearts" *(Jer 31:33)*. "I will put respect for me into their hearts, so that they turn from me no more. It will be my pleasure to bring about their good, and I will plant them firmly in this land with all my heart and soul" *(Jer 32:41)*. "See, the days are coming--it is Yahweh who speaks--when I am going to fulfill the promise I made to the House of Israel and the House of Judah: 'In those days and at that time, I will make a virtuous Branch grow for David, who shall practice honesty and integrity in the land ..." *(Jer 33:14-15)*. "If you are willing to remain peaceably in this country, I will build you and not overthrow you; I will plant you, not tear you up" *(Jer 42:10)*.

God the Just Judge

Jeremiah, like Isaiah, is moved by God to inform the nations that they, too, will not escape the effects of their injustice, brutality and arrogance. Chapters 46-51 speak of the punishments that await the Egyptians, Philistines, Moabites, Amonites, Edomites, Syrians, Arabian tribes and Babylonians: "All who pass by Babylon will be appalled at it and whistle in amazement at such calamity ... What! Broken to pieces that hammer of the whole world? What! Babylon become a thing of horror throughout the nations?" *(Jer 50:13,23)*.

EZEKIEL

Ezekiel's mission extended principally to the slaves exiled in Babylonia, although sections of his work speak to those still living in Jerusalem, both before and during the exile. His central message to all is the same: God demands inner conversion, conversion of heart, and not merely a change in outer behavior. Ezekiel's images of God mirror those of the other prophets, but they include his unique visions as well.

Ezekiel first recounts his awesome visions during the fifth year of the Jews' exile in Babylon. Yahweh appeared to him seated on a throne surrounded by brilliant light, his voice resounding like thunder, commissioning Ezekiel to bring his message to those still unconvinced of their guilt: "Warn them in my name. If I say to a wicked man: You are to die and you do not warn him, if you do not speak and warn him to renounce his evil ways and so live, then he shall die for his sin, but I will hold you responsible for his death. If however, you do warn a wicked man and he does not renounce his wickedness and his evil ways, then he shall die for his sin, but you yourself will have saved your life. When the upright man renounces his integrity to do evil ... he too shall die; since you failed to warn him, he shall die for his sin and the integrity he practiced will no longer be remembered; but I will hold you responsible for his death. If, however, you warn the upright man not to sin and he abstains from sinning, he shall live, thanks to your warning and you too will have saved your life" *(Ez 3:18-21)*.

The letter of James reflects this mission of Ezekiel: "My brothers, if one of you strays away from the truth and another brings him back to it, he may be sure that anyone who can bring back a sinner from the wrong way that he has taken will be saving a soul from death and covering up a great number of sins" *(Jas 5:19-20)*.

The responsibility to warn of sins and to encourage amendment recurs in Ezekiel, chapter 33, in which the prophet is compared to a sentry whose duty it is to watch and sound the alarm at the approach of the enemy.

God the Just Judge

Despite the siege of the Babylonians, the majority of the population in Jerusalem was in no mood for conversion. In God's wisdom the time for medicinal punishment had come, that some might be saved. "Since you do not keep my laws or respect my observances ... I will inflict punishments on you for all the nations to see ... a third of your inhabitants shall die of plague or starve to death inside you; a third shall fall by the sword outside you; a third I will scatter to every wind ..." *(Ez 5:7,8,12)*.

"But I shall spare some of you; they will escape the sword and be dispersed by me among the nations. Your survivors will remember me ... they will loathe themselves for all the wrong they have caused by their filthy practices and so they will learn that I am Yahweh ..." (*Ez 5:8-10*).

In chapter eighteen, Ezekiel addresses clearly the issue of personal responsibility before God. While the accumulated sins of people affect their nation adversely, exposing it to decay and eventual ruin, each person is accountable before God for his own sins only. Even here, however, God wants the sinner to live rather than to die. In accord with his great and merciful nature, God will forgive the repentant. In accord with his sense of justice, the unrepentant will experience the effects of their sins. "If the wicked man renounces all the sins he has committed, respects my laws and is law-abiding and honest, he will certainly live; he will not die. All the sins he committed will be forgotten from then on .... But if the upright man renounces his integrity, commits sin, copies the wicked man and practices every kind of filth, is he to live? All the integrity he has practiced shall be forgotten from then on; but this is because he himself has broken faith and committed sin and for this he shall die ... shake off all the sins you have committed against me and make yourselves a new heart and a new spirit! Why are you so anxious to die, House of Israel? I take no pleasure in the death of anyone--it is the Lord Yahweh who speaks. Repent and live!" (*Ez 18:21, 24, 31, 32;* also *33:10-20*).

Like Isaiah and Jeremiah, Ezekiel wants all people to know that the nations are only instruments of medicinal punishment for God's people. They, in their turn, will reap the whirlwind of their injustices. Chapters 25-32 speak of the punishments which await these nations.

God the Compassionate King

Chapter sixteen contains one of the most striking allegories of all the Scriptures. Yahweh is pictured as a wealthy king strolling through the fields who finds an abandoned newborn babe still wet with the blood of birth. Moved with compassion he takes the little girl home and cares for her as his very own daughter. He spares no expense in her upbringing, yet when she comes of age she becomes a whore and breaks his heart. His pleading fails to influence her to change her ways, so the king allows her to experience the consequence of her behavior in the hope that she will amend. But he never abandons his love for her. The allegory depicts Yahweh's mercy toward Israel, but it extends to every human being.

God the Gardener

In the following chapter Ezekiel pictures God taking a shoot from the top of a cedar, which he plants on a high mountain. There it flourishes, becoming a home for every kind of bird. The allegory immediately applies to the remnant of Israel that would be saved, but foreshadows the kingdom which Jesus would establish. When the nations see this phenomenon, they will recognize the awesome power of God. "Every tree of the field will learn that I, Yahweh, am the one who stunts tall trees and makes the low ones grow, who withers green trees and makes the withered green. I, Yahweh, have spoken, and I will do it" *(Ez 17:24)*.

Again in chapter nineteen God appears as a gardener planting a tender vine in fertile ground near a stream. The vine grows large and brings forth abundant fruit, until it proudly tries to touch the clouds (to act independently of God). Then men come and hack it down. They uproot the stem, exposing it to the sun. The shoots they plant in a desert wither and die. The allegory is directed to the succession of Israel's kings, whose reign will soon end. It applies to every son or daughter of God who turns away from him. The results are equally disastrous *(Ez 19:10-14)*.

God the Good Shepherd

After railing against the self-centered shepherds of his people, Yahweh says: "I am going to look after my flock myself and keep all of it in view ... I shall rescue them from wherever they have been

25

scattered during the mist and darkness ... and bring them back to their own land ... I shall feed them in good pasturage. They will browse in rich pasture ... I myself will show them where to rest ... I shall look for the lost one, bring back the stray, bandage the wounded and make the weak strong ... I shall be a true shepherd to them ... I mean to raise up one shepherd, my servant David, and to put him in charge of them and he will pasture them ... I, Yahweh, will be their God, and my servant David shall be their ruler" *(Ez 34:11-31)*. Here Ezekiel speaks obviously of a descendant of David, rather than of David himself. Christians understand Ezekiel's words as becoming fulfilled in Jesus, who referred to himself as the good shepherd *(Jn, 10)*.

God the Master of Life

Chapter 37 depicts one of the great awe-inspiring scenes of the Bible. Yahweh carries Ezekiel away in spirit and settles him in a valley full of human bones. These represent the death of hope in the exiled people of God. God then tells Ezekiel to prophesy new hope, new life. As he does so, the bones come together and grow sinews, muscle and skin. He calls for the breath of life to fill them. "I prophesied as Yahweh ordered me and the breath entered them; they came to life again and stood up on their feet, a great, an immense army" *(Ez 37:10)*. While scholars tell us that while this text cannot be used to prove the resurrection of all people — something Jesus later revealed to us — it does confirm that God has the power to restore life.

God the Beautiful Temple

Chapters 40-44 of Ezekiel describe a perfectly proportioned temple, beautifully adorned, where Yahweh promises to dwell here forever with those who love him and obey his laws. "I shall live here among the sons of Israel forever" *(Ez 43:7)*. The vision of a reconstructed temple was meant to fill the exiles with hope. The author of Revelation (21-22) uses the same image to encourage the persecuted early Christians. Ezekiel's images of God have not lost their power to encourage fidelity under trial.

DANIEL

Although the book of Daniel uses the setting of the Babylonian exile, Scripture scholars tell us that it was actually written during the persecution of the Jews under Antiochus Epiphanes, at about 160 years before the birth of Christ. The author's aim was to strengthen the faith of the Jews of his time by showing them that Daniel — with the help of Yahweh — had triumphed over similar ordeals. Though the tales may be fictitious, the book of Daniel offers us further insights into the wonderful God who made us all and who cares for us unceasingly.

God the Master of Knowledge

Nothing is unknown to God. Past, present, future are all the same to him. He is the source of knowledge and light. Happy are those enlightened by him. These truths are brought home in a clever way by the author of Daniel. He pictures Nebuchadnezzar, King of Babylon, being troubled by a dream which no one can interpret to the king's satisfaction. The king angrily condemns to death his sages.

Daniel, one of the Jewish exiles, asks to be given a chance to explain the dream, for Yahweh in a vision had explained its meaning to him. "May the name of God be blessed for ever and ever, since wisdom and power are his alone ... to confer wisdom on the wise and knowledge on those with wit to discern ... to know what lies in darkness ..." *(Dn 2:20-22)*. Gratified with this enlightenment, the king bestows a high rank and many gifts upon Daniel and his companions.

In chapter four the king has another confounding dream and once again Daniel, enlightened by Yahweh, reveals its meaning to him. "You are to be driven from human society and live with the wild animals; you will feed on grass like the oxen; you will be drenched by the dew of heaven ... until you have learned that the Most High rules over the kingship of men and confers it on whom he pleases" *(Dn 4:22)*. Moreover, in chapter fourteen, Cyrus of Persia, conqueror

27

of the Medes, is enlightened by Daniel (and Yahweh) concerning the deception of the priests of the god Bel *(Dn 14:1-22)*.

God the Savior

As the story progresses Daniel and his companions refuse to adore a golden statue which the king had presented as a god. This provokes the King's wrath and he orders them thrown into a burning furnace. "But the angel of the Lord came down into the furnace ... he drove the flames of the fire outward and fanned into them ... a coolness such as wind and dew will bring, so that the fire did not even touch them or cause them any pain or distress" *(Dn 3:49-50)*. The long song of Daniel and his companions praises the power and the mercy of God *(Dn 3:52-90)*. It is frequently used in the breviary, the church's official prayer book, on Sundays and Holy Days.

Another fascinating story of salvation, the famous rescue from the lions' den, occurs in chapter five. King Nebuchadnezzar and his son Belshazzar had both died and Darius, the Mede, then conquered the Chaldeans. Darius appointed 120 governors, one of whom was Daniel. The other governors hated Daniel and conspired to get rid of him by persuading Darius to sign an edict declaring himself a god, and forbidding prayer to any other god for thirty days. When Daniel refuses to obey this rule, they throw him into a pit of half-starved lions. Then Yahweh miraculously prevents the lions from harming him! The amazed Darius comes to realize the saving power of God as well as the treachery of his governors. He commands the governors to take Daniel's place in the pit and watches them devoured before his eyes.

A variation on the original story recurs in chapter fourteen, when the priests of the god Bel persuade King Cyrus to throw Daniel in the lions' den, again only to be rescued by God.

A third redemption story appears in chapter thirteen, concerning Susanna and the Corrupt Judges. The innocent Susanna entrusts her fate to God: "Eternal God, you know all secrets and everything before it happens; you know that they have given false evidence against me. And now have I to die, innocent as I am of everything their malice has invented against me?" *(Dn 13:43)*. God answers her by inspiring Daniel to question the two judges separately thus uncovering their lies. Susanna is saved and the people give glory to God: "the savior of those who trust in him" *(Dn 13:60)*.

God the Just Judge

The author of Daniel, like most of the other prophets, takes pains to show that arrogant nations, whom God allows to punish his people will not escape the effects of their sins. The punishment of these nations, which brings certain of them to their senses, appears in a series of visions *(Dn 8-14)*.

The reader of these visions, like Daniel, is apt to exclaim, "I listened but did not understand" *(Dn 12:8)*. But Yahweh answers that the full meaning will one day be revealed. However, the general meaning is already clear: suffering will bring some people to their senses, but those hardened in sin will not change. "Many will be cleansed, made white and purged; the wicked will go on doing wrong. The wicked will never understand; the learned will" *(Dn 12:10-11)*.

The message of the other Minor Prophets: Micah, Zephaniah, Nahum, Habakkuk, Haggai, Zechariah, Obadiah, Joel and Malachi, reflects this image of God.

The author of Jonah--in a masterfully woven tale--brings an important balance to this image. His story shows that God loves all people, not only the Jews. His mercy extends to all, for he is the father of all. Being a member of the Chosen People does not give anyone the right to despise others, or to rejoice in their misfortunes. God wants all of us to know him and be saved. "Am I not to feel sorry for Nineveh, the great city, in which there are more than a hundred and twenty-thousand people who cannot tell their right hand from their left..." *(Jn 4:11)*.

29

SECOND ISAIAH (Chapters 40-55)

This section of the Book of Isaiah was written by a different, unknown author, at some time toward the end of the Babylonian Exile. Scholars refer to it as "the Book of Consolation," for the author makes profound statements on how Yahweh intends to comfort and restore his people through a servant. The Jews identified this servant as Cyrus, the Persian, who would free them from Babylon. However, through faith, we believe the text to have a fuller meaning, referring to a servant who would console and restore all people to Yahweh. We believe the servant to be Christ, God-incarnate.

To see God as a servant can be unsettling to some people. Yet this is how Jesus looked upon himself and how he wishes us to view ourselves in relationship to the welfare of others. The image adds a fresh new dimension to previous understanding.

God the Triumphant Warrior

"Here is the Lord Yahweh coming with power, his arm subduing all things to him. The prize of his victory is with him, his trophies all go before him" *(Is 40:10)*.

God the Shepherd

"He is like a shepherd feeding his flock, gathering lambs in his arms, holding them against his breast and leading to their rest the mother ewes" *(Is 40:11)*.

God the Servant

"I have endowed him with my spirit that he may bring true justice to the nations ... He does not break the crushed reed nor quench the wavering flame ..." *(Is 42:1-2)*.

"I have appointed you ... to open the eyes of the blind, to free captives from prison" *(Is 42:7)*.

30

"Who could believe what we have heard ... like a sapling he grew up in front of us ... without majesty ... rejected by men ... familiar with suffering ... despised ... yet ours were the sufferings he bore, our the sorrows he carried. He was pierced through for our faults, crushed for our sins. On him lies a punishment that brings us peace and through his wounds we are healed. Harshly dealt with, he bore it humbly, he never opened his mouth, like a lamb that is led to the slaughterhouse, like a sheep that is dumb before its shearers ..." *(Is 53)*.

THIRD ISAIAH (Chapters 56-66)

This section contains a variety of prophecies from the pre- and post-periods of exile. Although the images of Yahweh as Savior and Just Judge are predominate in these chapters, the image of Yahweh the Mother appears near the end.

Yahweh the Mother

"Rejoice, Jerusalem, be glad for her, all you who love her! Rejoice, rejoice for her all you who mourned for her, that you may be suckled, filled, from her consoling breast .... At her breast will her nurslings be carried and fondled in her lap; like a son comforted by his mother will I comfort you" *(Is 66:10-13)*.

CHAPTER FOUR

IMAGES OF GOD IN THE PENTATEUCH

Several major Hebraic traditions serve as sources for the first five books of the Bible, which the Jews named the Torah. Scholars tell us that these traditions were combined and set down in writing only around 450 B.C. The Pentateuch arose from one central event: the Exodus, or liberation from slavery in Egypt, and the formation of the People of God in the Sinai desert, according to Yahweh's covenant.

The book of Genesis looks back to the patriarchal history of the Jews, adding some pre-historic legends about the human race. The book of Numbers elaborates on the desert journey of the Hebrews and their first settlements in Transjordan. The book of Leviticus details legislation to foster union with Yahweh. The book of Deuteronomy clarifies civil and religious laws for the People of God.

Flowing through the traditions of these books are a number of important images or understandings of God that remain helpful to those seeking the face of God.

GENESIS
God the Good Creator

The Priestly Tradition relates a poetic description of the creation of the world, based on the seven days of the week. Central to this tradition is the holiness and goodness of God, which he pours out on all creation. "In the beginning God created the heavens and the earth ... God saw all he had made and indeed it was very good" (Gn 1:1,31). "Yahweh fashioned man of dust from the soil. Then he breathed into his nostrils a breath of life and thus man became a living being ... Yahweh made the man fall into a deep sleep. And while he slept, he took one of his ribs and enclosed it in flesh. Yahweh built the rib he had taken from the man into a woman, and brought her to the man" (Gn 2:7, 21, 22).

God the Merciful Savior

The Yahwist Tradition centers on the instability of human beings, their attraction to sin and the effects of sin on individuals and society. Moreover, it highlights Yahweh's determination to save at least some of the human race from sin's evil effects. The kindness of God appears after the first sin in a mysterious promise of deliverance: "I will make you enemies of each other: you (the evil one) and the woman, your offspring and her offspring. It will crush your head and you will strike its heel" (Gn 3:15).

His mercy reappears when Yahweh marks Cain to inhibit others from killing him, as he did his brother, Abel. "So Yahweh put a mark on Cain to prevent whoever might come across him from striking him down" (Gn 4:15).

Yahweh spares the good Noah and his family from a flood which devastates the earth and its sin-laden population. "Go aboard the ark, you and all your household, for you alone among this generation do I see as a good man in my judgment" (Gn 7:1). "God blessed Noah and his sons, saying to them, 'Be fruitful, multiply and fill the earth" (Gn 9:1).

Similarly, Lot, another righteous man and nephew of Abram, is spared the awesome destruction of Sodom and Gomorrah. "When dawn broke the angels (messengers) urged Lot, 'Come take your wife and these two daughters of yours, or you will be overwhelmed in the punishment of the town ... run for your life. Neither look behind you nor stop anywhere on the plain. Make for the hills if you would not be overwhelmed'..." (Gn 19:15-18).

Yahweh also refuses to permit the sacrifice of Isaac, which Abraham believed God wanted him to make (Gn 22).

For the sake of his promise made to Abraham and his descendants, Yahweh spares Jacob the wrath of his brother Esau, whom Jacob had duped out of his birthright (Gn 25, 27, 32 and 33).

The sons of Jacob are spared death by famine through the mercy of their brother Joseph, whom they had sold into slavery, but also whom Yahweh had raised to greatness in Egypt (Gn 37, 39-48).

God the Kinsman

After choosing Abram to be the father of a people who would know Yahweh intimately and who would strive to follow his call to holiness, Yahweh--in a nomadic ritual of covenant--makes himself the clansman of Abram. In this ritual animals were killed and cut in two. Those intending to bind their lives and fortunes together walked between the slaughtered animals and in so doing told one another: *"May this happen to me, if I don't come to your aid in time of need."* In the dramatic story of chapter 15, only Yahweh passes as though shrouded through the divided animals. This act clearly indicated that he had chosen to become a kinsman of Abram, and would come to his defense and aid his posterity. "When the sun had set and darkness had fallen, there appeared a smoking furnace and a firebrand that went between the halves. That day Yahweh made a Covenant with Abram in these terms: 'To your descendants I give this land...'" (Gn 15:17-18).

Yahweh carries out his promise by bringing Abram under the protection of the Negeb desert king, Abimelech. The king also makes a covenant with Abram and shares his wealth with him (Gn 20,21).

EXODUS
God the Savior

In the book of Exodus Yahweh, the loyal kinsman, recognizes the plight of Abraham's offspring and comes to their aid. By his own power he frees them from the domination of the Egyptians, leads them out of slavery under the guidance of Moses and forms them into a new people called to lives of holiness. "I have seen the miserable state of my people in Egypt. I have heard their appeal to be free of their slave drivers. Yes, I am well aware of their suffering. I mean to deliver them out of the hands of the Egyptians and bring them up out of that land to a land rich and broad ..." (Ex 3:7-8).

"Moses stretched out his hand over the sea and, as the day broke, the sea returned to its bed. The fleeing Egyptians marched right into it and Yahweh overthrew the Egyptians in the very middle of the sea. The returning waters overwhelmed the chariots and the horsemen of Pharaoh's whole army, which had followed the Israelites into the sea; not a single one of them was left ... that day Yahweh rescued Israel from the Egyptians and Israel saw the Egyptians lying dead on the shore. Israel witnessed the great act that Yahweh had performed against the Egyptians and the people venerated Yahweh ..." (Ex 14:27-31).

God the Timeless One

We human beings are constantly measuring things to assess their value and greatness: the older, the more valuable; the more durable, the more valuable; the more powerful, the greater. Naming things instantly brings to mind their value and greatness: The Dead-Sea Scrolls, the Constitution, gold and diamonds, atomic energy and laser beams. At the request of his chosen servant, Moses, God reveals his name as Yahweh.

God's name gives some insight into his greatness. The Hebrew meaning of Yahweh is *I Am* ... I am timeless ... I have no beginning or end ... I am the fount of knowledge and power ... I am the source of all that is ... I am life itself ... I am goodness itself ... I am the one to whom all created things must answer. "God said to Moses, 'I Am who Am ... You are to say to the sons of Israel: Yahweh, the God of your fathers, the God of Abraham, the God of Isaac and the God of Jacob has sent me to you. This is my name for all time; by this name I shall be invoked for all generations to come...' " (Ex 3:14-15).

35

God the Wonder-worker

Chapters five to eleven recount a series of wonders. Yahweh works miracles through Moses to move the stubborn Pharaoh and deepen the Hebrews' faith in the power of God to liberate them. Whatever the ultimate explanation of those signs may be, the lesson is clear: God chose to intervene in human affairs in extraordinary ways in order to liberate his people from tyranny and extinction.

God the Lamb of Sacrifice

For a very long time, desert nomads had offered sacrifices of lambs and young goats to God to thank him for favors or to ask him for blessings. When Yahweh required this of the soon-to-be-liberated Hebrews, he wanted them to remember that it was he who liberated them; it was he who spared their first-born; it was he who looked upon the blood of the lamb and was moved to forgive them their infidelities. No one, of course, could comprehend that the roasted and eaten animals were only preparatory symbols of Yahweh's Son who would enter our world to become "the" sacrificial lamb that would liberate all people from slavery to sin, and who would nourish them on their way to the promised land. This was in the distant future of the Hebrews, but was ever present to Yahweh (Ex 12).

God the Water of Life

After the Hebrews had been liberated, they began a period of forty years of wandering in the desert. When their supplies gave out, they experienced thirst and hunger. Their fragile faith in Yahweh's providence was tested. They mistrusted him and complained bitterly about their lot. Again and again Yahweh forgave them and provided their needs. At Marah he made the bitter waters sweet (Ex 15:22-27). At Rephidim he provided water from a rock when Moses struck it with his rod (Ex 17).

The images of God as *Water of Life* and *Bread of Life* are of such major importance in the New Testament, that it seems proper here to

36

make a connection between them. Paul told the Corinthians that Christ was the spiritual rock that provided the water which they needed to survive. "They all drank from the spiritual rock that followed them them as they went and that rock was Christ" (I Cor 10:4).

Christ referred to himself as living water. Speaking to the Samaritan woman at the well of Sychar he said, "Whoever drinks this water will get thirsty again, but anyone who drinks the water that I shall give will never be thirsty again. The water that I shall give will turn into a spring inside him, welling up to eternal life" (Jn 4:13-14).

In the vision of a new and heavenly Jerusalem, the writer of the book of Revelation speaks of God slaking the thirst of all who dwell with him. "I will give water from the well of life free to anybody who is thirsty" (Rv 21:6). This recalls Ezekiel's vision of the life-giving stream which flows from the right side of the temple. "Wherever the water goes it brings health, and life teems wherever the river flows" (Ez 47:9).

God the Bread of Life

In order to assuage their hunger, Yahweh enabled the Hebrews to find a sweet, powdery and edible substance which they gathered and used as bread. Their exclamation, *Manna!* (What is this!) was used to recall their delight in the providential care of God while they roamed the desert wastes (Ex 16).

As Christ is the spiritual stream that slakes all peoples' thirst for insight into the very nature of God, so he is the "manna" which nourishes them with the power of God that they might be holy, as he is holy.

John developed this theme in chapter six of his gospel: Christ had recently fed about five-thousand men from a few loaves and fishes. The people wanted to make him king, so that they no longer would

37

have to struggle for survival. Christ used the occasion not only to correct their misconception about his mission, but also to clarify how he would help them attain holiness if they believed in and followed him. "I am the bread of life. He who comes to me will never be hungry; he who believes in me will never thirst ... I am the bread of life. Your fathers ate the manna in the desert and they are dead; but this is the bread that comes down from heaven so that a man may eat it and not die. I am the living bread which has come down from heaven. Anyone who eats this bread will live forever; and the bread that I shall give is my flesh, for the life of the world (Jn 6:35,48-51).

Through the gift of faith, we know that when we meet Christ in sacramental forms, especially in the Eucharist, he continues his work of sanctifying his people. The very life of God enters into us and gives us the power to put his teachings into practice that we might live forever. As Christ himself said: "It is the spirit that gives life; the flesh has nothing to offer. The words I have spoken to you are spirit and they are life" (Jn 6:63).

God the Kinsman

The covenant which Yahweh formed with Abraham, Isaac and Jacob he now renews with all the people liberated from Egypt. God promises that he will help them survive and prosper as a nation, but this time he makes the covenant conditional. The people must promise to obey the laws which Yahweh gives them through Moses. "You yourselves have seen what I did with the Egyptians, how I carried you on eagles' wings and brought you to myself. From this you know that now, if you obey my voice and hold fast to my covenant you, of all the nations, shall be my very own, for all the earth is mine. I will count you a kingdom of priests, a consecrated nation .... Then all the people answered as one: 'All that Yahweh has said we will do...'" (Ex 19:4-8).

38

God the Compassionate Lord

After Yahweh forgave the people's great sin of infidelity in worshiping the golden calf, Moses expressed his yearning to see Yahweh face-to-face. Yahweh replied: " I will let all my splendor pass in front of you and I will pronounce before you the name Yahweh. I have compassion on whom I will and I show pity to whom I please. You cannot see my face ... and live ... when my glory passes by, I will put you in a cleft of the rock and shield you with my hand while I pass by. Then I will take my hand away and you shall see the back of me; but my face is not to be seen ... Yahweh passed before him and proclaimed: 'Yahweh, Yahweh, a God of tenderness and compassion, slow to anger, rich in kindness and faithfulness; for thousands he maintains his kindness, forgives faults, transgression, sin; yet he lets nothing go unchecked, punishing the father's fault in the sons and in the grandsons to the third and fourth generation.'" (Ex 33:18-23, 34:6-7).

God the Cloud of Mystery and Power

When the Hebrews left Egypt the scriptures tell us that "Yahweh went before them, by day in form of a pillar of cloud to show them the way and by night in the form of a pillar of fire to give them light" (Ex 14:21).

From a dense cloud he gave them the Law. "Yahweh said to Moses, 'Come up to me on the mountain and stay there while I give you the stone tablets--the law and the commandments--that I have written for their instruction .... The cloud covered the mountain and the glory of Yahweh settled on the mountain of Sinai ..." (Ex 24:12,16).

Again, when the Tent of Meeting had been prepared, and all the vestments of the priests and utensils of worship had been fashioned, "the cloud covered the Tent of Meeting and the glory of Yahweh filled the tabernacle ... at every stage of their journey, whenever the cloud rose from the tabernacle the sons of Israel would resume their march. If the cloud did not rise, they waited and would not march until it did" (Ex 40:34-38).

LEVITICUS, NUMBERS, DEUTERONOMY

Leviticus, Numbers, and Deuteronomy all elaborate on the worship, struggles and laws of the Israelites. Central to all three books are specific images of Yahweh.

God the Supreme and Holy Ruler

The purpose of the holocausts, oblations and sacrifices demanded by the Law was to acknowledge the supremacy of Yahweh over all things (Lv 1-7 and Dt 12).

The consecration of men who would make the offerings, and even of the clothes they wore and the instruments they handled, stressed the holiness of God (Lv 8, 9, 21 and Nm 3, 8).

The separation of some foods into "clean" and "unclean," as well as the purifications of others also focused the attention of the people on the holiness of God and the holiness which he demanded (Lv 10-15).

"Yahweh spoke to Moses; he said: 'Speak to the whole community of the sons of Israel and say to them: Be holy, for I Yahweh your God, am holy'." (Lv 19:1-2 and Dt 14).

The penalties legislated for breaches of holiness--quite severe by modern standards but not for those primitive times--were enacted to constantly remind the people of Yahweh's demand for holiness. "You must keep my laws and put them into practice, for it is I, Yahweh, who make you holy" (Lv 20:8).

This demand for holiness is also stated as the reason for the "ban" or annihilation of populations that posed a threat to the moral life of the Israelites--a practice found in ancient times, but abhorrent to our developed concepts of morality. "You must lay them under the ban ... so that they may not teach you to practice all the detestable practices they have in honor of their gods and so cause you to sin against Yahweh, your God (Dt 20:17-18).

The rest and worship of the Sabbath, as well as the special feasts, celebrated the greatness and holiness of Yahweh (Lv 23 and Nm 28, 29 and Dt 15, 16).

Yahweh demanded that the lamp outside the veil of the Holy of Holies be kept burning to remind the priests of his holiness and their call to holiness (Lv 24).

God the Merciful Judge

Scattered throughout the books of Numbers and Deuteronomy are stories of complaints and rebellion against Yahweh and against his servant Moses. At the intercession of Moses, Yahweh forgives and does not punish the people as they deserve. Yahweh grants them food and drink in the wilderness (Nm 11:20), and he cures Miriam of leprosy (Nm 12). He pardons the rebellion of the tribes (Nm 14 and Dt 9), and he spares the community, while punishing Korah and his men (Nm 16). God cures those who gaze upon the fiery serpent on the standard (Nm 21), and also allows them to conquer the towns of Transjordan (Nm 21 and Dt 2:30 ff and 3). He also refuses to allow the seer, Balaam, to curse the Israelites (Nm 22-24). God abates the plague which afflicted the worshipers of Baal. "For Yahweh your God is a merciful God and will not desert or destroy you or forget the covenant he made on oath with your fathers" (Dt 4: 31 & Nm 25).

God the Faithful Lover

"If Yahweh set his heart on you and chose you, it was not because you outnumbered other peoples; you were the least of all peoples. It was for love of you and to keep the oath he swore to your fathers that Yahweh brought you out with his mighty hand and redeemed you

41

from the house of slavery, from the power of Pharaoh, King of Egypt. Know then that Yahweh your God is God indeed, the faithful God who is true to his covenant and his graciousness for a thousand generations toward those who love him and keep his commandments ... " (Dt 7:7-10).

The great love of God is the reason for all his gifts, laws and teaching. All God requires in return is our appreciation and obedience, not for his benefit, but for ours. We discover our dignity and the dignity of others, we achieve our greatness when we respond to his love, expressed in his teachings and directives. This is the essence of worship: remembering the love of God and responding to that love. That is why Yahweh commanded Moses to say: "You shall love Yahweh, your God, with all your heart, with all your soul, with all your strength. Let these words I urge on you today be written on your heart. You shall repeat them to your children and say them over and over again whether at rest in your house or walking abroad, at your lying down or at your rising; you shall fasten them on your hand as a sign and on your forehead as a circlet; you shall write them on the doorposts of your house and on your gates" (Dt 6:4-9).

The main message of Deuteronomy is: *don't forget God's love for you and respond to this love by following his commands*. "Take care you do not forget Yahweh your God, neglecting his commandments, customs and laws which I lay on you today" (Dt 8:11). This is the same message Jesus preached, as He fulfilled the law and prophets: "Anybody who receives my commandments and keeps them will be one who loves me; and anybody who loves me will be loved by my Father and I shall love him and show myself to him" (Jn 14:21).

CHAPTER FIVE

IMAGES OF GOD IN THE HISTORICAL BOOKS

The history of Scriptural writers is termed by scholars "interpretative history." They were not interested in recording historical events in the modern sense; rather they attempted to understand events which affected the life of the chosen people in terms of spiritual formulas which had predictable outcomes:

- Fidelity to Yahweh leads to victory and prosperity.
- Infidelity to Yahweh leads to defeat and poverty.
- Repentance leads to deliverance by Yahweh and new abundance.

Underlying and supporting this spiritual interpretation of history we find a number of images of God.

JOSHUA

When Moses was prohibited from entering the Promised Land (Nm 20:12), he appointed Joshua to the lead them in after his death. "Then Moses summoned Joshua and in the presence of all Israel said to him: 'Be strong, stand firm; you are going with this people into the land Yahweh swore to their fathers he would give them ... Yahweh himself will lead you; he will be with you. He will not fail you or desert you. Have no fear, do not be disheartened by anything" (Dt 31:7-8). These words reflect an understanding of Yahweh that dominates the Historical Books.

God the Victorious Leader

"Yahweh spoke to Joshua, son of Nun ... 'Moses my servant is dead; every place you tread I shall give you as I declared to Moses that I would ... no one shall be able to stand in your way. I will be with you as I was with Moses; I will not leave you or desert you.' " (Jos 1:1-5).

43

"Then Yahweh said to Joshua: 'Be fearless now and be confident ... I will put into your power the king of Ai, his people, his town and his territory.' " (Jos 8:1-2).

Concerning the Amorite kings Yahweh said to Joshua, "Do not be afraid of these men; I have delivered them into your power; not one of them will be able to stand against you" (Jos 10:8). "Yahweh drove them headlong before Israel, defeating them completely at Gibeon" (Jos 10:10).

As Joshua subdued king after king in the south the text reads: "All these kings and their kingdoms Joshua mastered in one campaign, because Yahweh, the God of Israel, fought for Israel" (Jos 10:42).

When his victories were repeated in the north, the sacred writer boasts: "Yahweh delivered them into the power of Israel, who defeated them and pursued them ... harried them till not one was left to escape" (Jos 11:8).

JUDGES

When Joshua died, central leadership died as well. The Book of Judges recounts the exploits of certain tribal leaders called judges, who continued the battle to settle the land. Although the Book of Joshua gave the impression that the whole land was conquered, apportioned and settled, the Book of Judges shows us that in fact, this was not the case. The book's central message is clear: infidelity to Yahweh leads to defeat; repentance to deliverance. The image of Yahweh as the merciful judge is all-pervasive.

God the Merciful Judge

Chapter one shows that the tribes disobeyed the orders of Yahweh. A messenger from Yahweh states, "You have not obeyed my orders ... very well, I now say this: I am not going to drive out these nations

44

before you. They shall become your oppressors and their gods shall be a snare for you" (Jgs 2:3).

The sacred writer relates how the fertility gods of Baal and Astarte had captivated the minds of the people, dividing their hearts and making them easy prey for their enemies. He also says, "Yahweh appointed judges for them. Yahweh was with the judge and rescued them from the hands of their enemies as long as the judge lived, for Yahweh felt pity for them as they groaned under the iron grip of their oppressors" (Jgs 2:18).

The king of Edom enslaved them for eight years. When they cried for mercy, they were freed by the judge, Othniel, and lived in peace for forty years (Jgs 3:7-11).

The king of Moab enslaved them for eighteen years. The judge, Ehud, freed them and ushered in an eighty-year period of peace (Jgs 3:12-30).

The king of Canaan enslaved them for twenty years, until the judge and prophetess, Deborah, finally defeated him, enabling the people to enjoy another forty years of peace (Jgs 4, 5).

The kings of Midian enslaved them for seven years. Yahweh chose the farmer, Gideon, to liberate them. But to make it clear that it was Yahweh, and not Gideon or his men who had done this, he reduced their fighting men from 32,000 to 300. "There are too many people with you for me to put Midian into their power; Israel might claim the credit for themselves at my expense. They might say: 'My own hand has rescued me.' " (Jgs 7:2). Gideon's victory then brought another forty years of peace.

The Ammonites dominated the Israelites for eighteen years. When they pleaded for mercy, Yahweh sent them Jephthah as a savior (Jgs 10-12).

When the Israelites relapsed again, Yahweh permitted the hated Philistines to enslave them for forty years, until he raised up Samson to destroy the Philistine leaders (Jgs 13-16).

Set in the hard and cruel times of the Judges, the story of Ruth is a beautiful story of compassion. The image of a merciful and kind God shines through the brief tale. Naomi, the mother-in-law of Ruth, is moved by Ruth's love and also by the assistance of Boaz to exclaim: "May he be blessed by Yahweh who does not withhold his kindness from the living or dead!" (Ru 2:20).

I AND II SAMUEL

The two books of Samuel conclude the story of the Judges and introduce the period of the Kings of Israel. As in the foregoing, the image of Yahweh as a merciful judge prevails throughout Samuel I and II.

God the Merciful Judge

God hears and grants the request of Hannah for a child, who becomes the great Judge and Prophet, Samuel (1 Sm 1-3).

When their archenemies, the Philistines, again defeat Israel and capture the ark, Yahweh has mercy on his people by afflicting the Philistines until they return it, but he permits them to harass the unfaithful Israelites for another twenty years until Samuel intercedes for them (1 Sm 4-7).

God grants the Israelites a king, although their request impugns his leadership. Through Samuel, he warns them of the burdensome effects of their choice (1 Sm 8).

He enables the new king, Saul, to score a resounding victory over the Ammonites, but warns the people and king to be faithful to him or

46

perish (1 Sm 9-12).

Saul repeats his victory over the Philistines and Amalekites, but does not follow Samuel's directives and finds himself rejected as king (1 Sm 13, 15).

Yahweh's new choice is a shepherd lad called David. Saul, unaware of this selection of David, calls him into his service, because of his reported skills on the harp and his reputation as a fighter. When David kills Goliath, the giant warrior of the Philistines, with his sling and is praised by the maidens of Israel, jealousy begins to consume Saul. "The women sang: 'Saul has killed his thousands and David his tens of thousands.' His jealousy led him to make several attempts on David's life. But Yahweh is with David and protects him from harm (1 Sm 16-23).

Yahweh's mercy moves David to spare the life of Saul. "Your own eyes have seen today how Yahweh put you in my power in the cave and how I refused to kill you, but spared you. I will not raise my hand against my lord, for he is the anointed of Yahweh" (1 Sm 24:11 and 26).

As the first book of Samuel comes to an end, the mercy of God enables David to find favor with the Philistines to whom he fled to avoid the wrath of Saul. God's mercy also protects him from the wrath of his own people, who blamed him for the slaughter of their people by the Amalekites (1 Sm 27-30).

After the death of Saul (1 Sm 31) and a period of mourning (2 Sm 1), David begins his battle for recognition as king of the tribes of Israel. After several battles, he is crowned king at the age of 30. He begins a reign of 40 years: 7 years over Judah and 33 years over Judah and Israel (2 Sm 2-5). Yahweh's promise of deliverance from the hated Philistines is now fulfilled. "David did as Yahweh had ordered and routed the Philistines from Gibeon as far as the pass of Gezer" (2 Sm 5:25).

47

God the Loving Father

During a rare period of peace, David expressed a desire to build a temple for Yahweh. Nathan, the prophet, replied: "Yahweh will make you great; he will make you a House. And when your days are ended and you are laid to rest with your ancestors, I will preserve the offspring of your body after you and make his sovereignty secure ... I will be a father to him and he a son to me; if he does evil, I will punish him with the rod such as men use ... yet I will not withdraw my favor from him, as I withdrew it from your predecessor. Your House and your sovereignty will always stand secure before me and your throne be established forever" (2 Sm 7:12-16).

At one point, David's faith in the promise of Yahweh becomes tested. When his lust drives him to send Uriah to his death that he might have Uriah's wife, Bathsheba, Yahweh rebukes David through Nathan, but he does not reject him. No amount of David's pleading, however, saves the child born of his illicit union. Internal strife is also forecast for the House of David, because of his disloyalty (2 Sm 10-12). One of David's sons, Amnon, rapes David's daughter, Tamar. In outrage, another brother, Absalom, kills him and then flees from the wrath of David (2 Sm 13). Five years later, when his anger had cooled, David forgives his son (2 Sm 14), only to have Absalom plot the overthrow of his father and then establish himself as king. But so strong is Absalom's popularity that David must flee for his life (2 Sm 15).

During his flight he is cursed by a common man. Absalom further shames him by sleeping with David's concubines (2 Sm 16). Even when Absalom's plans of attack are revealed to David (2 Sm 17) and his army defeated by David's troops, David's order that Absalom's life be spared is not obeyed (2 Sm 18), and Absalom's death rends David's heart (2 Sm 19). Even when a fragile peace is reestablished with the tribes, occasional revolts continue (2 Sm 20). A famine also afflicts the country for three years, while the Philistines reorganize and wage a series of wars on the House of David (2 Sm 21).

48

God the Rock and Fortress of Salvation

The terrible events in David's life destroyed neither his faith in Yahweh's wisdom nor his belief in Yahweh's providential care of him. They served only to deepen it.

Chapter 22 recounts the image of Yahweh that dominated the thoughts of David as he approached his death. "Yahweh is my rock and my bastion, my deliverer ... my support ... my lamp ... my salvation. Yahweh ... you are faithful with the faithful, blameless with the blameless, pure with the pure, but crafty with the devious; you save a people that is humble and humiliate eyes that are haughty ... the word of Yahweh is without dross ...." If only God would grant us such depth of faith and trust!

I AND II KINGS

The First Book of Kings begins with the last days of David and his transfer of power to Solomon, who would build the temple and bring the nation to its apex of power. As the books end, we see the temple destroyed, the nation in ruins and the people deported to Babylon. As might be expected, a variety of images of Yahweh are found in the books.

Even the transfer of power does not come easily to David. As Absalom tries to supplant David as king, so Absalom's brother, Adonijah, tries to preempt David's appointment of Solomon as king. His ploy comes too late, however. David hurriedly appoints his son, Solomon, who after David's death, takes revenge, not only on Adonijah and his supporters, but also on all those who had insulted or betrayed his father. With all opposition crushed, the text says: "And now the sovereignty was securely in the hands of Solomon" (1 Kgs 1-2).

God the Wise King

Yahweh speaks to Solomon in a dream and encourages him to ask for whatever he would. Solomon requests an understanding and wise heart. "Give your servant a heart to understand how to discern between good and evil, for who could govern this people of yours that is so great?" The request pleases Yahweh: "I give you a heart wise and shrewd as none before you has had and none will have after you. What you have not asked, I shall give you too: such riches and glory as no other king ever had. And I will give you a long life, if you follow my ways, keeping my laws and commandments ..." (1 Kgs 3:9-14).

This wisdom is thus exemplified: in Solomon's decision on the true mothers of the living and dead babes (1 Kgs 3:16-28); in his appointment of good administrators (1 Kgs 4); in his composition of songs and proverbs and knowledge of nature (1 Kgs 5); and particularly in his construction and beautification of the temple and palace (1 Kgs 5:5ff, 6-7). His prowess in business is the envy of the Gulf. Even the queen of Sheba travels to Jerusalem to learn from him (1 Kgs 10).

God the Merciful Judge

Prosperity eventually swells the pride of Solomon, making him deaf to the mandates of Yahweh and blind to the misery of his people, who felt crushed by his taxation and imposition of labor.

The deafness appeared in his fondness for foreign wives, a custom forbidden by Yahweh. "You are not to go to them nor they to you or they will surely sway your hearts to their own gods" (1 Kgs 11: 2). He commanded his builders and artisans to build shrines to house the gods.

Punishment came swiftly "Since you behave like this and do not keep my covenant or the laws I laid down for you, I will most surely tear the kingdom away from you and give it to one of your servants. For your father David's sake, however, I will not do this during your lifetime, but will tear it out of your son's hands. Even so, I will not tear the whole kingdom from him. For the sake of my servant David, and for the sake of Jerusalem, which I have chosen, I will leave your son one tribe" (1 Kgs 11:11-13).

Clouds of war and internal strife gathered on the horizon before the death of Solomon. Hadad had stirred up the Edomites, Rezon captured Damascus, and Jeroboam turned ten of the tribes against Solomon, before fleeing to Egypt. After Solomon's death, the storm broke with fury. Rehoboam, the son and successor of Solomon, lacked the most elementary form of wisdom: the ability to listen. To an appeal for a lighter load of labor and taxation he replied: "My father made you bear a heavy burden. I will make it heavier still. My father beat you with whips; I am going to beat you with loaded scourges." To this unfeeling and harsh reply the leaders of the people replied: "What share have we in David? We have no inheritance in the son of Jesse. To your tents, Israel! Henceforth look after your own house, David!" They stoned the king's envoy, while the king himself fled (1 Kgs 12:14-16).

As Rehoboam mustered forces in Jerusalem to punish the tribes of Israel, the leaders gathered around Jeroboam, who had returned secretly from Egypt. Having been warned by the holy man, Shemaiah, not to fight against Jeroboam, Rehoboam resigns himself to a split kingdom. "Yahweh says this: Do not go to fight against your brothers, the sons of Israel; let everyone go home, for what has happened is my doing" (1 Kgs 12:24).

This political split affected the total life of the people. For the Israelites it would mean gradual alienation from Yahweh. Since they could not (and would not) go to Jerusalem for worship, the Israelites demanded their own temples, and two of these were constructed, one in the north (Dan) and one in the South (Bethel). Jeroboam instituted his own line of priests to serve them (1 Kgs 12:26 and 13). The

51

sacred author observes: "Such conduct made the House of Jeroboam a sinful House and caused its ruin and extinction from the face of the earth" (1 Kgs 13:34). Scholars tell us that the remarks were inserted later, when the ten tribes were conquered by Assyria and disappeared in the forced slave deportation to Nineveh.

Sensing his opportunity in this split, Shishak, the king of Egypt, invaded Jerusalem and despoiled the temple and palace, leaving Rehoboam a broken and powerless king (I Kgs 14).

Rehoboam and Jeroboam were succeeded by a whole line of weak and sinful kings. The sacred authors do not mention a single good king in Israel. They find only two of merit in Judah: Hezekiah and Josiah. Elijah and the other prophets rail against the injustices of these sinful leaders and foretell dire punishments awaiting the kingdoms of Judah and Israel, because of their infidelity to Yahweh. Accordingly the unrepentant kings look on the prophets as irritants and scourges. "When he saw Elijah, Ahab said: 'So there you are, you scourge of Israel!' 'Not I,' he replied, 'I am not the scourge of Israel, you and your family are; because you have deserted Yahweh and gone after the Baals.' " (I Kgs 18:17-18).

God the Gentle Breeze

While hiding from the wrath of Jezebel, Ahab's wife, Elijah is favored with an encounter with Yahweh. Near the mountain of Horeb "Yahweh himself went by. There came a mighty wind, so strong it tore the mountains and shattered the rocks ... but Yahweh was not in the wind. After the wind came an earthquake, but Yahweh was not in the earthquake. After the earthquake came a fire, but Yahweh was not in the fire. After the fire there came the sound of a gentle breeze. When Elijah heard this, he covered his face with his cloak and went out and stood at the entrance of the cave" (I Kgs 19:11-13).

The Second Book of Kings continues this sad tale of infidelity and injustice. The phrase "He did what is displeasing to Yahweh" like a refrain, is repeated over and over again. Consequently, the land becomes afflicted with famine, kings are assassinated, royal families are massacred and war is now a fact of life. The widespread sinfulness of leaders and people makes it impossible for them to experience the blessings of peace and gentleness that Yahweh wished to bestow.

The kingdom of Israel was the first to collapse. "The king of Assyria invaded the whole country and coming to Samaria, laid siege to it for three years. In the ninth year of Hosea, the prophet, the king of Assyria captured Samaria and deported the Israelites to Assyria ... this happened because the Israelites had sinned against Yahweh ... they worshiped other gods, they followed the practices of the nations that Yahweh had dispossessed for them. The Israelites, as well as the kings they had made for themselves, plotted wicked schemes against their God. And yet through all the prophets, Yahweh had given Israel and Judah this warning: "Turn from your wicked ways and keep my commandments; but they would not listen ... they pursued emptiness ... Yahweh was enraged with Israel and thrust them away from him. There was none left but the tribe of Judah only" (2 Sam 17:5-18).

The tribe of Judah also had to experience two deportations to Babylon before it realized the folly of its infidelity to Yahweh, the God who only wanted good things for them.

CHRONICLES, EZRA AND NEHEMIAH

Chronicles, Ezra and Nehemiah reflect the experience of the Exile and were written by a single author about three centuries after Cyrus, the Persian, had conquered Babylon and permitted the Jews to return to their homeland. They encourage new trust and dependency on Yahweh and they also emphasize the importance of listening to his word as recorded in the Scriptures and as explained by the teachers. The image of God which stirred the author reflects that of his predecessors.

God the Faithful Kinsman

The two books of Chronicles review the history of the Chosen People and show their survival, despite the unfaithfulness of the leaders and people. The unspoken conclusion is that Yahweh has lived up to his promise; he deserves to be listened to and obeyed. The wise understand this and prosper, the foolish are doomed to repeat the mistakes of the past. "Yahweh is with you so long as you are with him. When you seek him, he lets you find him; when you desert him, he deserts you. Many a day Israel will spend without a faithful God, without priests to teach, without law; but in their distress they will return to Yahweh, the God of Israel; they will seek him and he will let them find him. When that time comes, no grown man will know peace, for many troubles will afflict all the inhabitants of the country. Nation will be shattered by nation, city shattered by city, since God will afflict them with every kind of distress. But for your part, take courage, do not let your hands weaken, for your deeds will be rewarded" (2 Chr 15:2-7).

The two good kings of Judah, Hezekiah and Josiah, are presented as models of faith and reform (2 Chr 29-35). Hezekiah's message was: "Do not be stubborn now as your ancestors were. Yield to Yahweh ... serve Yahweh ... for Yahweh is gracious and merciful. If you come back to him, he will not turn his face from you" (2 Chr 30:8-9).

The Book of Ezra commences with Cyrus's decree of liberation. It describes the opposition experienced by the Jews from the current occupants of the land, who used political intrigue to prevent them from rebuilding the temple or the walls of Jerusalem. The prophets Haggai and Zechariah encouraged the returnees to persevere and not to lose heart. Finally, under Darius, the Persian, a decree of Cyrus was uncovered which had given permission for the construction of a temple. Darius ratified the permission and work began. His successor, Artaxerxes, later gave permission to rebuild the walls. The Book of Nehemiah celebrates these two events and the providential care of Yahweh. It also encourages the people to be faithful to the

54

covenant established with their ancestors and renewed with them. "All the people gathered as one man on the square before the Water Gate. They asked Ezra, the scribe, to bring the Book of the Law of Moses which Yahweh had prescribed for Israel.

Accordingly Ezra the priest brought the Law before the assembly ... he read from the book from early morning till noon; all the people listened attentively to the Book of the Law ... then Ezra blessed Yahweh the great God and all the people raised their hands and answered: Amen! Amen!; then they bowed down and, face to the ground, prostrated themselves before Yahweh" (Neh 8:1-6).

TOBIT, JUDITH AND ESTHER

Three pious and stirring tales, *Tobit, Judith* and *Esther,* are often included under the Historical Books because of their historical settings. However, scholars tell us that they were actually written between the 2nd and 4th centuries, B.C.

The purpose of each author is to edify, instruct and encourage, rather than merely to pass on historical data. Each book transmits its particular image of Yahweh to the reader.

God the Merciful Judge

Challenging the religious indifference and social callousness of the Third-century Jews, the author of Tobit created a pious tale set in the time of the Assyrian Exile.

Tobit, a God-fearing and charitable Jew, is accidentally blinded (Tb 1-3). He sends his son, Tobias, to recover some money from Gabael in Media. Before setting out, however, Tobias meets a messenger from Yahweh, who offers to accompany him. The messenger tells Tobias how to prepare an eye ointment from the gall of a fish and protects him and his new wife, Sarah, from harm. On returning home,

Tobias applies the ointment to Tobit's eyes and the old man recovers his sight. He rejoices to see his son and Sarah. During a feast of thanks the messenger reveals his identity and disappears (Tb 4-12).

All give thanks to Yahweh: "Blessed be God who lives for ever, for his reign endures throughout all ages! By turns he punishes and pardons; he sends men down to the depths of the underworld and draws them up from supreme destruction; no one can escape his hand ... Though he punishes you for your iniquities, he will take pity on you all ... if you return to him with all your heart and all your soul behaving honestly toward him ... he will return to you and hide his face from you no longer" (Tb 13:1-6).

God the Savior

The Book of Judith was composed during the war-torn Maccabean Period, around 150 B.C. Although the story is religious fiction (recognized by the incompatible events and personages) its purpose was to stir up hope of deliverance from current Greek oppressors and from all future ones as well.

The heroine of the story, Judith, relies on Yahweh to help her overcome the Assyrian warlord, Holofernes, who had come to ravage Israel and Judah. Her trust is not misplaced, for after beguiling Holofernes with her womanly charms, she beheads the wine-sodden warrior in his tent. When she displays his head to the Israelites, they find the courage they need to attack and overcome the Assyrians. After the victory they praise Judith and she praises Yahweh: "The Lord is a God who shatters war; he has pitched his camp in the middle of his people to deliver me from the hands of my enemies ... Lord, you are great, you are glorious, wonderfully strong, unconquerable .... Woe to the nations who rise against my race! The Lord Almighty will punish them on judgment day..." (Jdt 16:2, 13, 17).

The Book of Esther, another colorful tale, deepens the Chosen

People's faith in the saving power of Yahweh. Predating the Book of Judith, it provided the Jews with a colorful story for their Feast of Purim or Lots on which they recall the downfall of racist plotters.

In the story Haman, chief officer of King Ahasuerus of Persia, is driven by hatred of Mordecai, the Jew, to persuade the king to issue a decree of extermination against all the Jews. Unbeknown to Haman, the king's new queen, Esther, is herself a Jew who had been raised by Mordecai. As the fateful day of doom draws near, Mordecai approaches Esther and asks her to intercede on behalf of their race. Esther begs strength from Yahweh: "My Lord, our King, the Only One, come to my help, for I am alone and have no helper but you ... give me courage, King of Gods and Master of all Power. Put persuasive words into my mouth when I face the lion; change his feeling into hatred for our enemy that the latter and all like him may be brought to their end ... save us from the hand of the wicked and free me from my fear" (Est 4:3, 12, 19). Her prayer is heard. She braves a death penalty by entering the king's chamber without being summoned. The king spares her and listens to her request that he and Haman attend a banquet which she has been preparing. When they come, Esther invites the two of them to a another, more intimate feast. Here she begs for her life and that of her people. When the king discovers his decree would mean the death of his queen, he leaves the room to ponder. In his absence Haman flings himself on Esther and begs for mercy. As he does so, the king reenters and believing Haman to be attacking his queen, summons his guards, who drag Haman away. The decree of extermination is nullified. Haman is hung on a scaffold he had built for Mordecai, along with his collaborators. They then celebrate with a feast this occasion of salvation from the wicked who hate God's People.

BARUCH

Some scholars put the Book of Baruch in the prophetic section of Scripture. Although its setting is the Babylonian Exile, scholars know that it was written by an unknown author of the second century, claiming to be Baruch, the scribe of Jeremiah. This was a common technique, used by ancient writers to attract the listener's attention.

The author's purpose was to encourage the Jews of his time to turn their backs on lifeless idols and to worship the living God, who chose to dwell in a special way in the temple of Jerusalem. The work is a classic in biblical satire.

God the Living Lord

In the beginning of the book the author highlights the root cause of the Exile: the Chosen People's infidelity to Yahweh and their trust of empty idols. "We have been disloyal ... we have taken to serving alien gods and doing what is displeasing to the Lord our God" (Bar 1:20-22).

His satire begins in chapter three, where he asks: "Where now are the leaders of the nations ... those who displayed such artistry in silver that their masterpieces beggar imagination? They have vanished ..." (Bar 3:16-19).

It hits full stride in chapter six, where he ridicules the worshipers of idols that cannot do anything for themselves or others. "Plated with gold and silver ... they are counterfeit and have no power to speak ... cannot protect themselves either from tarnish or woodworm ... powerless to defend themselves against war or thieves ... eyes full of dust ... gnawed from within by termites ... faces blackened by smoke ... don't be afraid of them" (Bar 6: 54-72).

The implied message is clear: the Chosen People must fear and obey and worship the Living Lord of Heaven and Earth!

I AND II MACCABEES

In the fifth century, B.C. political power shifted from Persia to

Greece. While Greek generals conquered land after land, Greek enthusiasts tried to impose their philosophy and culture on the conquered nations. When Palestine came under their control, this posed a serious danger to the Chosen People, for many of them found Greek philosophy and culture very attractive. To complicate matters, King Antiochus IV, who tried to Hellenize the Jews by force, found that many of the Jewish leaders were only too happy to help him.

The first book of Maccabees describes the revolt of the zealot, Mattathias and his sons, against this state of affairs. His guerrilla wars proved successful. The temple was then cleansed and rededicated, and a feast commemorated the event, called Hannukah (Feast of Lights).

God the Wise Law-Giver

Mattathias and his sons looked upon Yahweh as the glory of Israel. The Law he gave his people epitomizes wisdom. Those who follow it become wise and good. To turn one's back on it and on the worship that keeps it constantly before one's mind represents the height of foolishness and disloyalty, a betrayal of the history of the Chosen People and a mockery of all their religious heroes.

The second book of Maccabees reviews and elaborates on the events of first Maccabees for the Jews living in Egypt. By describing the persecution and suffering of those loyal to Yahweh, the sacred author encourages pride in their noble heritage and faithfulness to the Law. He also shows the final outcome of the struggle to be on the side of those faithful to Yahweh.

God Merciful Judge

The second book of Maccabees is unique in that it affirms belief in a future life. Judas Maccabeus had a collection taken up and sent to Jerusalem to have sacrifices offered for soldiers who had died in battle. The sacred author comments on his action: "An altogether fine and noble action, in which he took full account of the resurrection. For if he had not expected the fallen to rise again it would have been superfluous and foolish to pray for the dead, whereas if he had in view the splendid recompense reserved for those who make a pious end, the thought was holy and devout. This was why he had this atonement sacrifice offered for the dead, so that they might be released from their sin" (2 Mc 12: 43-45).

CHAPTER SIX

IMAGES OF GOD IN THE WISDOM WRITINGS

Most of these writings were composed during the Greek Period of Jewish history, and represent a reaction to the attraction exercised by the Hellenists on the Hebrews throughout their empire.

Hebrew scholars had blended a number of ancient traditions into an accepted version of the Torah, which was now widely used by Jews living both in and outside of Palestine. These writings of wisdom highlighted the beauty of the Torah, the blessings that occurred when it was lived, and the disastrous results that followed when it was ignored. The three periods of exile in Egypt, Assyria and Babylon play a big part in this literature, as does the prophets' call to repent and to obey Yahweh. The wise man, in the mind of the sacred writers, always obeys Yahweh. The fool disobeys him. To seek wisdom through other gods, through human philosophies, through practices opposed to those revealed by Yahweh, is so much chasing after wind. It leads to dishonor, shame and death. The wise man, on the other hand, by meditating on God's word day and night, finds honor, happiness and life.

The question of life beyond death also plays a major role in the wisdom literature. The early works contain no clear and satisfying answer. However, the conviction that God rewards the good person and punishes the evil one remains, as does the conviction that he never abandons the just person. Only in the book of Wisdom (written about 50, B.C.) is the immortality of the human spirit finally affirmed.

The wisdom writings offer a rich variety of images of God. Many of these are found in the Psalms, on which we've already reflected. The other books: Job, Proverbs, Ecclesiastes (Qoheleth), Ecclesiasticus (Ben Sirach), the Song of Songs and Wisdom have their own unique contributions to make in helping us "see" the God we love.

61

JOB

In the literature of Mesopotamia, Egypt and Greece, the lives and fortunes of men and women were at the whims of the gods. These fickle gods sometimes sent prosperity to unjust people and suffering to good people. The author of Job rejects this notion, while exploring the question of the suffering of good and innocent people.

The author employs the literary form of religious drama, which centers on a debate carried out in poetic dialogue. Job, the central character, was probably an historic figure known principally for his patience, but the drama and debate are contrived to teach profound religious truths.

Eliphas, Bildad and Zophar are characters who defend the traditional answers to suffering. The goodness of Yahweh is never questioned, only why he permits evil people to prosper and good persons to suffer. Lacking a special revelation about a life after death, the author has Yahweh rebuke Job's lack of understanding, terminate his suffering, and restore his fortunes to justify him before his friends.

God the Wise Master

"His heart is wise and his strength is great: who then can successfully defy him? He moves the mountains ... He and no other stretched out the skies ... His works are great, beyond all reckoning ... " (Jb 9:4,5,10). "You modeled me, as clay is modeled ... then you endowed me with life, watched each breath of mine with tender care" (Jb 10:9,12). "He holds in his power the soul of every living thing, and the breath of each man's body" (Jb 12:10). "He said to man: Wisdom? It is fear of the Lord. Understanding? It is avoidance of evil" (Jb 28:28).

PROVERBS

The book of Proverbs offers astute observations on human affairs. While many of them echo the maxims of the ancient world of Mesopotamia and Egypt, the sacred writer organizes them around a central theme: obedience to Yahweh and to the Law makes a person wise. The maxims themselves then become individual applications of how to do this in the particular circumstances of life. They are to be meditated on one at a time.

The sacred writer did not have the benefit of a revelation about a future life. He, like the author of Job, expects full compensation for goodness in this life. He also yearns for the punishment of evil people in this life. Although some of the maxims are no longer applicable or valid, the majority of them still offer helpful insights and advice on human behavior. They also promote respect for life and order in society.

God the Wise Father

"The fear of Yahweh is the beginning of knowledge ..." (Prv 1:7). "Yahweh himself is giver of wisdom ... he keeps his help for honest men ... he keeps watch on the way of his devoted ones" (Prv 2:6-8).

"My son, do not forget my teaching, let your heart keep my principles, for these will give you lengthier days, long years of life and greater happiness. Let kindliness and loyalty never leave you; tie them around your neck and write them on the tablet of your heart. So shall you enjoy favor and good repute in the sight of God and man. Trust wholeheartedly in Yahweh ... do not think of yourself as wise; fear Yahweh and turn your back on evil ... honor Yahweh with what goods you have ... do not scorn correction from Yahweh, for Yahweh reproves the man he loves as a father checks a well-loved son" (Prv 3:1-12).

"My son, hold to sound judgment and to prudence, do not let them out of your sight; they will prove the life of your soul, an ornament around your neck ... do not refuse a kindness to anyone who begs it, if it is in your power to perform it. Don't say to your neighbor: Go away! Come another time! I will give it to you tomorrow! if you can do it now" (Prv 3:27-28).

"Listen my son, take my words to heart ... hold fast to discipline, never let her go ... never set your foot on the path of the wicked ... more than all else, keep watch over your heart, since here are the well-springs of life" (Prv 4:10-23).

"My son ... take no notice of a loose-living woman ... find joy with the wife you married in your youth ... the adulterer has no sense; act like him and court your own destruction" (Prv 5:7-23).

"I, Wisdom, ... hate pride and arrogance, wicked behavior and a lying mouth. I love those who love me; those who seek me eagerly shall find me" (Prv 8:1,13,17).

ECCLESIASTES (QOHELETH)

Ecclesiastes in Hebrew means *the Preacher*. In contrast with the author of Job, who debates the problem of suffering, the Preacher is concerned with happiness ... happiness in this world, because he is not enlightened by the revelation of an existence after death.

The Preacher directs his message to his contemporaries who were abandoning their beliefs for Hellenistic fables and worship in the hope of achieving perfect happiness. While the Preacher yearns and hopes for complete happiness, he leaves the reader with the feeling that complete human happiness is illusory. Nevertheless, obedience and loyalty to Yahweh will bring the greatest measure possible. Leaving him leads to sorrow, not joy.

The author used a literary form known as meditative monologue.

64

There is no logical unity to the Preacher's musings, but he delights in using contradictory proverbs that should never be isolated from the context. Nevertheless, his words challenge both heart and mind.

God the Wise Giver

"There is no happiness for man but to eat and drink and to be content with his work. This I see as something from God's hand ... wisdom, knowledge, joy he gives to the man who pleases him; on the sinner lays the task of gathering and storing up for another who is pleasing to God" (Eccl 3:24-26). "When man eats and drinks and finds happiness in his work, this is a gift of God" (Eccl 3:13).

"I know very well that happiness is reserved for those who fear God, because they fear him and that there will be no happiness for the wicked man and that he will only eke out his days like a shadow, because he does not fear God. But there is a vanity found on earth: The good, I mean, receive the treatment the wicked deserve and the wicked the treatment the good deserve" (Eccl 8:12-14).

"Go, eat your bread with joy and drink your wine with a glad heart, for what you do God has approved beforehand ... Spend your life with the woman you love, through all the fleeting days of the life that God has given you under the sun; for this is the lot assigned to you in life and in the efforts you exert under the sun. Whatever work you propose to do, do it while you can, for there is neither achievement, nor planning, nor knowledge, nor wisdom in Sheol where you are going" (Eccl 8:7-10).

ECCLESIASTICUS (SIRACH)

Greek versions of this book called it *The Wisdom of Ben Sirach*. His advice is similar to that of the author of Proverbs; however, he also eulogizes the wise men of the Hebrews to make the Jews of his time proud of their heritage and heroes.

65

The book was a favorite of the early Christian communities, who read it frequently. Accordingly, it picked up the name *The Church's Book* (Ecclesiasticus in Latin).

God the Wise Creator

Wisdom: "God himself has created her, looked on her and assessed her, and poured her out on all his works to be with all mankind as his gift and he conveyed her to those who love him ... to fear the Lord is the root of wisdom and her branches are long life" (Sir 1:9,10,20).

"My son, if you aspire to serve the Lord ... be sincere of heart, be steadfast and do not be alarmed when disaster comes. Cling to him and do not leave him, so that you may be honored at the end of your days. Whatever happens to you accept it, and in the uncertainties of your humble state, be patient, since gold is tested in the fire and chosen men in the furnace of humiliation. Trust him and he will uphold you and follow a straight path and hope in him ... wait for his mercy ... who ever trusted in the Lord and was put to shame ... was left forsaken ... was ignored?" (Sir 2:1-12).

"My son, be gentle in carrying out your business ... a stubborn heart will come to a bad end ... almsgiving atones for sins ... do not refuse the poor a livelihood ... don't avert your eyes from the destitute ... return the poor man's greeting courteously ... be like a father to orphans and as good as a husband to widows" (Sir 3:17,26,30 and 4:1,5,8,10).

"My son, bide your time and be on your guard against evil ... Do not show partiality ... do not refrain from speech at an opportune time ... Do not be ashamed to confess your sins ... Fight to the death for truth and the Lord God will war on your side ... Do not be like a lion at home ... Do not give your heart to money ... Do not be led by your appetites and energy to follow the passions of your heart ... Be quick to listen and deliberate in giving an answer ... Do not give in to the promptings of your temper in case it gores your soul like a mad bull.

Prayer to Our Mother of Perpetual Help

Mother of Perpetual Help, you have been blessed and favored by God. You became not only the Mother of the Redeemer, but Mother of the redeemed as well. We come to you today as your loving children. Watch over us and take care of us. As you held the child Jesus in your loving arms, so take us in your arms. Be a mother ready at every moment to help us. For God who is mighty has done great things for you, and God's mercy is from age to age on those who love God. Intercede for us, dear Mother, in obtaining pardon for our sins, love for Jesus, final perseverance, and the grace always to call upon you, Mother of Perpetual Help. Amen.

Perpetual Help Center
Redemptorist Fathers of New York

294 EAST 150TH STREET • BRONX, NY 10451-5195
TEL: (718) 585-3678 • FAX: (718) 993-5870
WWW.PERPETUALHELPCENTER.ORG

12190PC

Our Mother of Perpetual Help,

Pray for Us.

Let your acquaintances be many but your advisers one in a thousand ... A faithful friend is a sure shelter, whoever finds one has found a rare treasure ... Reflect on the injunctions of the Lord, busy yourself at all times with his commandments. He will strengthen your mind and the wisdom you desire will be granted you" (Sir 5:20ff and 6:2,6,14,36,37).

"Happy the man who has not sinned in speech ... who meditates on wisdom, who studies her ways ... and ponders her secrets ... whoever fears the Lord will act like this and whoever grasps the Law will obtain wisdom ... He will find happiness and a crown of joy; he will inherit an everlasting name" (Sir 14:1,20,21 and 15:1).

"Next, I will remind you of the works of the Lord ... by the words of the Lord his works come into being and all creation obeys his will ... Not a thought escapes him, not a single word is hidden from him ... The sun, as he emerges, proclaims: A thing of wonder is the work of the Most High ... the moon, always punctual ... the stars makes the beauty of the sky ... the rainbow ... drawn by the hands of the Most High ... his treasuries open and the clouds fly out like birds ... He sprinkles snow like birds alighting ... who can glorify him as he deserves?" (Sir 42-43).

"Next let us praise illustrious men ... Enoch pleased the Lord. Noah was found perfectly virtuous. Abraham ... no one was ever his equal. Moses ... beloved by God and men ... God gave him commandments for his people and showed him something of his glory. Aaron, a holy man, like Moses. Phinehas ... stood firm when the people revolted. Joshua, a great savior. Caleb, devoted to service. Samuel, loyal and beloved of his Lord. David gave thanks to the Holy One. Solomon, wise in his youth. Elijah, glorious in miracles. Isaiah revealed the future. Josiah set his heart on the Lord" (Sir 44-49).

"Happy is he who busies himself with these things and grows wise by taking them to heart. If he practices them he will be strong enough for anything, since the light of the Lord is his path" (Sir 50:28-29).

THE SONG OF SONGS

The Song of Songs is a series of love poems. The title indicates that they are the most beloved of all the love poems ever written, because they speak of Yahweh's love for his people and the love of God's People for Yahweh.

In the poems the lovers speak to one another about their deep feelings. These are expressed in love terms of the ancient Near East and may not be fully appreciated by people of different cultures. Still, the general message is clear: Yahweh deeply loves his people and will never forget them, while those who love Yahweh long to see him and hear his voice.

God the Lover

The Bridegroom: "How beautiful you are, my love ... as a lily among thistles ... without a blemish ... You ravish my heart ... What spells lie in your love ... My love is unique, mine, unique and perfect ... How beautiful you are, how charming, my love, my delight ... Set me like a seal on your heart, like a seal on your arm ... love no flood can quench, no torrents drown."

The Bride: "You will be our joy and our gladness. We shall praise your love above wine ... How beautiful you are, my Beloved and how delightful ... Come then, my lovely one, come ... I am my Beloved's and my Beloved is mine. He pastures his flock among the lilies ... I am my Beloved's and his desire is for me..." (Sg 1-8).

WISDOM

Wisdom is the last composed book of the Old Testament. It was written by a Greek-speaking Hebrew, who attributed it to Solomon in order to entice the attention of his readers.

With the other sacred authors of this period, he seeks to strengthen the faith of the Chosen People in Yahweh and to thwart the efforts of the Hellenists. To do this effectively, he emphasizes the joy that comes from union with Yahweh. The breakthrough feature of this joy is that it is not restricted to this life, but extends to a life beyond the grave.

Chapters One to Five speak of the destiny of good and evil persons. Chapters Six to Nine warn arrogant leaders of ultimate destruction and encourage conversion. Chapters Ten to Nineteen use the Exodus to show how God protects good people, but afflicts the foolish with the very things they abuse.

God the Just Judge

"The souls of the virtuous are in the hands of God. No torment shall ever touch them. In the eyes of the unwise, they did appear to die, their going looked like a disaster, their leaving us, like annihilation; but they are in peace ... They shall judge nations, rule over peoples, and the Lord will be their king for ever. They who trust in him will understand the truth. Those who are faithful will live with him in love, for grace and mercy await those he has chosen ... But the godless will be duly punished for their reasoning, for neglecting the virtuous man and deserting the Lord" (Wis 3:1-3,8-10).

"The hope of the godless is like chaff carried on the wind, like fine spray driven by the gale ... but the virtuous live forever, their recompense lies with the Lord. The Most High take cares of them" (Wis 5:14-15).

"The Lord does not cower before a personage; he does not stand in awe of greatness, since he himself has made small and great and provides for all alike. But strict scrutiny awaits those in power" (Wis 6:7-8).

"What man indeed can know the intentions of God? Who could have

69

learned it, had you not granted Wisdom and sent your holy spirit from above. Thus have the paths of those on earth been straightened and men been taught what pleases you, and saved by Wisdom" (chp. 6, vrs. 7-8).

CHAPTER SEVEN

IMAGES OF GOD REVEALED BY JESUS

The many images of God revealed to us in the Old Testament help us to appreciate just how good and wonderful God is. They continue to have great meaning, even though the Son of God has appeared in the flesh. Jesus himself can be seen in many different ways: as a teacher, friend, wonderworker, good shepherd, prophet, father, as well as others. In fact, as we read the Gospels we find that Jesus actually refers to God and himself in very picturesque language.

Each image, like a piece of a mosaic, or a segment of a stained-glass window, adds some beauty to and understanding of the marvelous Being we human beings call God. Each image helps us to better understand Jesus. Each image has its own impact on our minds and emotions. Each image has its part to play in the different stages of our lives. Each image has its particular appeal and challenge at certain important moments in our lives. Each image, therefore, is a gift from God, to help us on our journey to the place where we will, one day, see him face to face.

These images and the all-too-brief stories of Jesus fill our hearts with joy, but also create in us a desire for greater understanding and intimacy. We can discover further insights and grow in intimacy if we spend quiet time with our loving Father and with Jesus, the one he has sent to help us.

Jesus the Teacher

Perhaps the most dominant image of Jesus in all the Gospels is that of teacher, although the image of healer runs a close second. Jesus is pictured as teaching:
- in the synagogue (Lk 4:15),
- in the temple (Lk 19:47 and Jn 7:14),
- by the lake of Galilee (Mk 4:1),

71

- on the hillside (Mt 5:1),
- in towns (Mt 11:1) and villages (Mk 8:27),
- in private homes (Lk 5:29ff.).

His disciples referred to him as "Rabbi," which means teacher:
- "Rabbi, where do you live?" (Jn 1:38).
- "Rabbi, you are the Son of God" (Jn 1:49).
- "Rabbi, we know you are a teacher who comes from God" (Jn 3:2).
- "Rabbi, it is wonderful for us to be here!" (Mk 9: 5).
- "Look, Rabbi, the fig tree you cursed has withered away" (Mk 11:21).
- "Rabbi, have something to eat" (Jn 4:31).
- "Rabbi, when did you come here?" (Jn 6:26).
- "Rabbi, who has sinned, this man or his parents?" (Jn 9:2).
- "Rabbi ... are you going back again?" (Jn 11:8).
- "Rabbuni (My teacher) let me see again!" (Mk 10:51).
- "Rabbuni!" (Cried by Mary of Magdala) (Jn 20:17).

The teachings of Jesus that are passed on to us are not all-inclusive. Indeed, the evangelist John says that if he tried to record everything, the world could not hold the books that would need to be written (Jn 20:31). However, the little that is recorded helps us to believe in Jesus and to walk the way that leads to life. Here are some issues on which Jesus, the teacher, sheds light:

His role was to fulfill, not destroy the Law or the teachings of the Prophets. "Do not imagine that I have come to abolish the Law or the Prophets. I have not come to abolish, but to complete them" (Mt 5:17).

The heart of the Law and Prophetical teachings is: Obedience to God leads to life. "If you wish to enter into life, keep the commandments" (Mt 19:17).

The first and greatest commandment is: love God and neighbor as yourself. "You must love the Lord your God with all your heart, with all your soul, with all your mind and with all your strength. The second is this: You must love your neighbor as yourself. There is no commandment greater than these" (Mk 12:28-32). These words reflected the teachings of Deuteronomy (Dt 8:4-5) and Leviticus (Lv 19:18).

Even enemies are to be loved. "Love your enemies and pray for those who persecute you; in this way you will be sons of your Father in heaven, for he causes his sun to rise on bad men as well as good and his rain to fall on honest and dishonest men alike" (Mt 5:38-48, Lk 6:27-35 and 10:29-37).

If we expect to have our sins forgiven, we must forgive. "Forgive us our debts, as we have forgiven those who are in debt to us" (Mt 6:12).

"If your brother does something wrong, reprove him and if he is sorry, forgive him. And if he wrongs you seven times a day and seven times comes back to you and says, 'I'm sorry,' you must forgive him" (Lk 17:3-4).

Revenge is anti-Christian. Jesus rebuked James and John for their desire to punish the Samaritan village which refused to receive them (Lk 9:51-56).

A person is not justified by ritual acts, but by keeping his heart free of evil intentions. "From the heart come evil intentions: murder, adultery, fornication, theft, perjury, slander. These are the things that make a man unclean. But to eat with unwashed hands does not make a man unclean" (Mt 15:19-20).

The greatest person in the eyes of God is the one who considers himself the least (a child) and serves the rest. "If anyone wants to be first, he must make himself last of all and servant of all" (Mk 9:33-37, Lk 9:46-48 and 22:24-27).

Happiness is found by the poor in spirit, the gentle, those who mourn over evil, those who hunger and thirst for goodness, the merciful, the pure in heart, the peacemakers, those who suffer persecution for the sake of Christ (Mt 5:1-12, Lk 6:20-23).

Unshared riches pose an obstacle to salvation. "I tell you solemnly, it will be hard for a rich man to enter the kingdom of heaven" (Mt 19:23-26, Mk 10:23-27, Lk 18:24-27). "Fool! This very night the demand will be made for your soul; and this hoard of yours, whose will it be then?" (Lk 12:13-21). "No servant can be the slave of two masters ... You cannot be the slave both of God and of money" (Lk 16:1-15). "There was a rich man ... and at his gate there lay a poor man called Lazarus ... who longed to fill himself with the scraps that fell from the rich man's table" (Lk 16:19-31).

Whatever is given to the poor or by the poor is treasured by God and will be rewarded. "Sell your possessions and give alms. Get yourselves purses that do not wear out, treasure that will not fail you in heaven where no thief can reach it and no moth destroy it" (Lk 12:33-34). "A poor widow came and put in two small coins ... I tell you solemnly, this poor widow has put more in than all who have contributed to the treasury, for they have all put in money they had over, but she from the little she had has put in everything she possessed, all she had to live on" (Mk 12:41-44, Lk 21:1-4). "Be careful not to parade your good deeds before men to attract their notice ... your almsgiving must be secret and your Father who sees all that is done in secret will repay you" (Mt 6:1-4).

Governmental laws (which include payment of taxes) are to be observed without detriment to God's laws. "Give back to Caesar what belongs to Caesar, and to God what belongs to God" (Mt 22:15-22, Lk 20:20-26).

Prayer is helpful when it is sincere, not done for show, and when it relies on God's Providence. "Do not imitate the hypocrites; do not babble as the pagans ... pray like this: Our Father in heaven ..." (Mt

6:1-15, Lk 11:1-13). "Will not God see justice done to his chosen who cry to him day and night even when he delays to help them?" (Lk 18:1-8).

Fasting is helpful, again if it is sincere. "When you fast, put oil on your head and wash your face so that no one will know you are fasting except your Father who sees all that is done in secret; and your Father who sees all that is done in secret will reward you" (Mt 6:16-18).

Divorce of one's spouse is contrary to God's plan for marriage. "I say this to you: the man who divorces his wife--I'm not speaking of fornication--and marries another is guilty of adultery ... and if a woman divorces her husband and marries another she is guilty of adultery too" (Mt 19:1-9, Mk 10:1-12, Lk 16:18).

Those who scandalize the innocent will be punished severely. "Obstacles indeed there must be. Alas for the man who provides them" (Mt 18:5-10, Mk 9:42-50, Lk 17:1-3).

Faithful use of one's talents in the service of God will be rewarded. "Happy that servant if his master's arrival finds him at his employment. I tell you truly, he will place him over everything he owns" (Lk 12:35-48). "I tell you, to everyone who has, more will be given; but from the man who has not, even what he has will be taken away" (Lk 19:11-27).

Salvation demands repentance and submission to God. "Unless you repent you will all perish as they did" (Lk 13:1-4). "Try your best to enter by the narrow door, because I tell you many will try to enter and will not succeed" (Lk 13:22-30). "Anyone who does not carry his cross and come after me cannot be my disciple" (Lk 14:25-27). "Watch yourselves, or your hearts will be coarsened with debauchery and drunkenness and the cares of life ... stay awake, praying at all times for the strength to survive all that is going to happen ..." (Lk 21:34-36).

God loves the humble and rejects the proud. "Everyone who exalts himself will be humbled and the man who humbles himself will be exalted" (Lk 14:7-11). "This man (the tax-collector) I tell you, went home again at rights with God; the other (the Pharisee) did not" (Lk 18: 9-14).

Jesus, of course, shed light on many more things than those mentioned above. He taught us about the inner life of God (the Trinity), about his Father, his Spirit, about his kingdom and the means of entering it and fostering it. He taught us the inner meaning of his parables. He unveiled the mystery of life after death and the state of those who love and hate him (heaven and hell). In fact, Jesus taught by everything he said and did. The more we reflect on his life and words, the clearer they become and the more they affect our lives.

Jesus the Healer

The most appealing picture we have of Jesus is that of healer, healer of body and spirit. The words, "And he healed him ... he healed her ... he healed them" permeate all the gospels like an enchanting refrain of a song.

God wants us to be well, to be whole, to be happy. While not all illnesses and sufferings come from sin, a lot of sickness, disunity, unhappiness is self-inflicted, or caused by others who are dominated by sin. By sending his Son into our world of sin and suffering, God wants us to know that he cares. By helping those who appealed to him with faith, Jesus wanted them to know that he cared. By sending out his followers to help the sick and suffering in his name, his message of caring extends to those who can no longer come to him physically.

As you spend time with each of the marvelous stories of healing which the gospels record, you can't help feeling the tender love of our compassionate God. His love has inspired, and continues to inspire,

76

countless men and women to reach out to those who are suffering in body or spirit to help them find the healing they want so badly.

Besides the stories of individual healings which the gospels record, we are told several times that Jesus healed all who came to him:

"That evening they brought to him many who were possessed by devils. He cast out the spirits with a word and cured all who were sick. This was to fulfill the prophecy of Isaiah: 'He took our sicknesses away and carried our diseases for us.' " (Mt 8:16-17, Mk 1:32-34, Lk 4:40-41).

"Jesus made a tour through all the towns and villages, teaching in their synagogues, proclaiming the Good News of the kingdom and curing all kinds of diseases and sickness" (Mt 9:35).

"He took them (the Twelve) with him and withdrew to a town called Bethsaida where they could be by themselves. But the crowds got to know and they went after him. He made them welcome and talked to them about the kingdom of God. And he cured those who were in need of healing" (Lk 9:10-11).

"Having made the crossing, they came to land at Gennesaret. When the local people recognized him they spread the news through the whole neighborhood and took all that were sick to him, begging him just to let them touch the fringe of his cloak. And all those who touched it were completely cured" (Mt 14:34-36, Mk 6:53-56).

"Jesus went on from there and reached the shores of the Sea of Galilee and he went up into the hills. He sat there and large crowds came to him bringing the lame, the crippled, the blind, the dumb and many others; these they put down at his feet, and he cured them. The crowds were astonished to see the dumb speaking, the cripples whole again, the lame walking and the blind with their sight and they praised the God of Israel" (Mt 15:29-31).

"There were also blind and lame people who came to him in the Temple and he cured them. At the sight of the wonderful things he did and of the children shouting: 'Hosanna to the Son of David' in the Temple, the chief priests and scribes were indignant" (Mt 21:14-15).

These cited passages are certainly stirring. However, the stories of individual healings are even more moving. Checking over the Gospels we find two tales of the healing of lepers, three of the raising of dead people to console their loved ones, four of the curing of possessed or mentally afflicted persons and eleven other individual stories of people who were made whole again.

Leprosy was and is a dreaded disease. In the time of Jesus the disease was not only irreversible, but entailed exclusion from the community. Lepers were truly the living dead. Who can fail to be touched by the simple stories of their cures?

"After Jesus had come down from the mountain large crowds followed him. A leper came up and bowed low in front of him. 'Sir,' he said, 'if you want to, you can cure me.' Jesus stretched out his hand, touched him and said: 'Of course I want to! Be cured!' And his leprosy was cured at once" (Mt 8:1-3, Mk 1:40-42, Lk 5:12-14).

"Now on the way to Jerusalem Jesus traveled along the border between Samaria and Galilee. As he entered one of the villages, ten lepers came to meet him. They stood some way off and called to him: 'Jesus, Master! Take pity on us!' When he saw them he said: 'Go and show yourselves to the priests.' Now as they were going away they were cleansed. Finding himself cured, one of them turned back praising God at the top of his voice and threw himself at the feet of Jesus and thanked him" (Lk 17:11-16).

The loss of a loved one can be almost as devastating as being rejected by society. The pain will not subside. No distraction works. The heart feels the void and will not be compensated by any consolation. Like a gaping wound, it refuses to heal quickly or to close. Jesus understood this agony, and on three occasions he decided to end it for some very fortunate people.

"One of the synagogue officials came up, Jairus by name, and seeing Jesus, fell at his feet and pleaded with him earnestly, saying: 'My little daughter is desperately sick. Come and lay your hands on her to make her better and save her life' ... While he was still speaking some people arrived from the house of the synagogue official to say:' Your daughter is dead' ... They came to the official's house ... Jesus went in and said to them: 'Why all this commotion and crying? The child is not dead but asleep.' They laughed at him ... Taking with him the child's father and mother and his own companions, he went into the place where the child lay. Taking the child by the hand he said to her: 'Talitha, kum!' which means 'Little girl, I tell you get up!' The little girl got up at once and began to walk about for she was twelve years old" (Mk 5:21-43, Mt 9:18-26, Lk 8:40-56).

"Jesus went to a town called Naim, accompanied by his disciples and a great number of people. When he was near the gate of the town it happened that a dead man was being carried out for burial, the only son of his mother and she was a widow. A considerable number of the townspeople were with her. When the Lord saw her he felt sorry for her. 'Do not cry,' he said. Then he went up and put his hand on the bier and the bearers stood still. He said: 'Young man, I tell you get up.' And the dead man sat up and began to talk and Jesus gave him to his mother" (Lk 7:12-17).

"On arriving, Jesus found that Lazarus had been in the tomb for four days already. Bethany is only about two miles from Jerusalem and many Jews had come to Martha and Mary to sympathize with them over their brother ... At the sight of her (Mary's) tears and those of the Jews who followed her, Jesus said in great distress, with a sigh that came straight from the heart: 'Where have you put him?' They said, 'Lord come and see.' Jesus wept; and the Jews said: 'See how much he loved him!' ... Jesus said: 'Take the stone away.' He cried out in a loud voice: 'Lazarus, Come out!' The dead man came out, his feet

and hands bound with bands of stuff and cloth around his face. Jesus said to them: 'Unbind him; let him go free.' "
(Jn 11:1-44).

While persons who have been born blind may not miss sight, those who have enjoyed this gift, and lost it, feel excruciating pain. Jesus felt their pain and healed those who faithfully appealed to him.

"As they left Jericho a large crowd followed him. Now there were two blind men sitting at the side of the road. When they heard that it was Jesus who was passing by they shouted: 'Lord! Have pity on us, Son of David.' ... Jesus stopped, called them over and said: 'What do you want me to do for you?' They said to him, 'Lord, let us have our sight back.' Jesus felt pity for them and touched their eyes and immediately their sight returned and they followed him" (Mt 20:29-34).

"As Jesus went on his way (through Galilee) two blind men followed him shouting: 'Take pity on us, Son of David.'... Jesus said to them: 'Do you believe I can do this?' They said: 'Sir, we do.' Then he touched their eyes saying: 'Your faith deserves it, so let this be done for you.' And their sight returned" (Mt 9:27-31).

"They came to Bethsaida and some people brought to him a blind man, whom they begged him to touch. He took the blind man by the hand and led him outside the village. Then putting spittle on his eyes and laying his hands on him he asked: 'Can you see anything?' The man, who was beginning to see, replied: 'I can see people; they look like trees to me, but they are walking about.' Then he laid his hands on the man's eyes again and he saw clearly. He was cured and he could see everything plainly and distinctly" (Mk 8:22-26).

"As he left Jericho with his disciples and a large crowd, Bartimaeus, a blind beggar, was sitting at the side of the road. When he heard that it was Jesus of Nazareth he began to shout: 'Son of David, Jesus, have pity on me.'... Jesus stopped and said: 'Call him here.' So they called

80

the blind man ... So throwing off his cloak, he jumped up and went to Jesus. Then Jesus spoke: 'What do you want me to do for you?' 'Rabbuni,' the blind man said to him, 'Let me see again.' Jesus said to him: 'Go. Your faith has saved you.' And immediately his sight returned and he followed him along the road" (Mk 10:46-52).

In the Gospel of John we are given a lengthy account of the healing of a man who was born blind. Here are a few excerpts from the story: "As he went along, he saw a man who had been blind from birth. His disciples asked him: 'Rabbi, who sinned, this man or his parents, for him to have been born blind?' 'Neither he nor his parents sinned,' Jesus answered. 'He was born blind so that the works of God might be displayed in him.'... Having said this, he spat on the ground, made a paste with the spittle, put this over the eyes of the blind man, and said to him, 'Go and wash in the Pool of Siloam.' So the blind man went off and washed himself, and came away with his sight restored" (Jn 9:1-7).

Next to blindness, most people dread losing their mind. Insanity in ancient times was thought to be a result of demonic possession. Some of the Gospel accounts seem to take this approach. Even epilepsy was attributed to satanic take-over. Whether these people suffered from actual possession or a deterioration of their faculties, or from some disease, their plight touched the heart of Christ, moving him to liberate them from their bondage.

"When he reached the country of the Gadarenes on the other side (of Lake Genesaret) two demoniacs came toward him out of the tombs--creatures so fierce that no one could pass that way. They stood there shouting: 'What do you want with us, Son of God!'... The devils pleaded with Jesus: 'If you cast us out, send us into the herd of pigs.' And he said to them: 'Go, then.' They came out and made for the pigs; and at that the whole herd charged down the cliff into the lake and perished in the water" (Mt 9:28-34, Mk 5:1-20, Lk 8:26-39).

"In their synagogue (of Capernaum) there appeared a man possessed by an unclean spirit. It shouted: 'What do you want with us, Jesus of Nazareth?'... Jesus said sharply: 'Be quiet! Come out of him!' And the unclean spirit threw the man into convulsion and with a loud cry went out of him" (Mk 1:21-28, Lk 4:33-37).

"They were coming down from the mountain when a large crowd came to meet him. Suddenly a man in the crowd cried out: 'Master,' he said, 'I implore you to look at my son. He is my only child. All at once a spirit will take hold of him and give a sudden cry and throw the boy into convulsions with foaming at the mouth; it is slow to leave him, but when it does, it leaves the boy worn out.'... Jesus said in reply ... 'Bring your son here.' The boy was still moving toward Jesus when the devil threw him to the ground in convulsions. But Jesus rebuked the unclean spirit and cured the boy and gave him back to his father and everyone was awestruck by the greatness of God" (Lk 9:37-43, Mt 17:14-18, Mk 9:14-29).

"They (the two cured blind men) had only just left when a man was brought to him, a dumb demoniac. When the devil was cast out, the dumb man spoke and the people were amazed" (Mt 9:32-34 and 12:22-24).

Each of the eleven personal stories of healing which the Gospels relate further reinforce our understanding of the compassion of God. "When Jesus went into Capernaum a centurion came up and pleaded with him. 'Sir,' he said, 'my servant is lying at home paralyzed and in great pain.' 'I will come myself and cure him,' said Jesus. The centurion replied, 'Sir, I am not worthy to have you under my roof; just give the word and my servant will be cured.' ... To the centurion Jesus said: 'Go back, then; you have believed, so let this be done for you.' And the servant was cured at that moment (Mt 8:5-13, Lk 7:1-10).

"On leaving the synagogue, Jesus went with James and John straight to the house of Simon and Andrew. Now Simon's mother-in-law had gone to bed with fever and they told him about her straightaway. He went to her, took her by the hand and helped her up. And the fever left her and she began to wait on them" (Mk 1:29-31, Mt 8:14-15, Lk 4:38-39).

"Now on another Sabbath Jesus went into the synagogue and began to teach and a man was there whose right hand was withered ... He said to the man with the withered hand, 'Stand up! Come out into the middle.' And he came out and stood there. Jesus looked around at them all and said to the man: 'Stretch out your hand.' He did so, and his hand was better" (Lk 6:6-11, Mt 12:9-14, Mk 3:1-6).

"A Canaanite woman from that district (Tyre and Sidon) started shouting, 'Sir, Son of David, take pity on me. My daughter is tormented by a devil.' ... The woman had come up and was kneeling at his feet. 'Lord,' she said, 'help me.' Then Jesus answered her, 'Woman, you have great faith. Let your wish be granted.' And from that moment her daughter was well again" (Mt 15:21-28, Mk 7:24-30).

"There was a woman suffering from a hemorrhage for twelve years, whom no one had been able to cure. She came up behind him and touched the fringe of his cloak and the hemorrhage stopped at that instant ... 'My daughter,' he said, 'your faith has restored you to health; go in peace.' " (Lk 8:43-48, Mt 9:20-22, Mk 5:25-34).

"He was teaching one day ... when some men appeared, carrying on a bed a paralyzed man whom they were trying to bring in and lay down in front of him. But as the crowd made it impossible to find a way of getting him in, they went up on to the flat roof and lowered him and his stretcher down through the tiles into the middle of the gathering, in front of Jesus ... He said to the paralyzed man: 'I order you: Get up and pick up your stretcher and go home.' And immediately before their very eyes he got up, picked up what he had been lying on and went home praising God" (Lk 5:17-26).

"One sabbath day Jesus was teaching in one of the synagogues and a woman was there who for eighteen years had been possessed by a spirit that left her enfeebled; she was bent double and quite unable to stand upright. When Jesus saw her he called her over and said: 'Woman, you are rid of your infirmity,' and he laid his hands on her. And at once she straightened up and she glorified God" (Lk 13:10-13).

"Jesus had gone for a meal to the house of one of the leading Pharisees ... There in front of him was a man with dropsy and Jesus addressed the lawyers and Pharisees: 'Is it against the law to cure on the Sabbath, or not?' They remained silent, so he took the man and cured him and sent him away" (Lk 14:1-6).

"There was a court official whose son was ill at Capernaum and hearing that Jesus had arrived in Galilee from Judaea, he went and asked him to come and cure his son, as he was at the point of death .... 'Go home,' said Jesus. 'Your son will live.' The man believed what Jesus had said and started on his way. While he was still on the journey back, his servants met him with the news that his boy was alive. He asked them when the boy had begun to recover. 'The fever left him yesterday,' they said, 'at the seventh hour.' The father realized that this was exactly the time when Jesus had said, 'Your son will live.' And he and all his household believed" (Jn 4:47-53).

"Jesus went up to Jerusalem. Now at the Sheep Pool in Jerusalem there is a building ... consisting of five porticoes. Under these were crowds of sick people ... One man there had an illness which had lasted thirty-eight years ... Jesus said: 'Do you want to be well again?' 'Sir,' replied the sick man, 'I have no one to put me into the pool when the water is disturbed.' ... Jesus said: 'Get up, pick up your sleeping mat and walk.' The man was cured at once and he picked up his mat and walked away" (Jn 5:1-9).

These touching gospel stories climax with the healing of a man who had come to apprehend him. "Jesus' followers, seeing what was happening, said: 'Lord, shall we use our swords?' And one of them struck out at the high priest's servant (Malchus) and cut off his right ear. At this Jesus spoke. 'Leave off!' he said. 'That will do!' And touching the man's ear, he healed him" (Lk 22:47-51).

Jesus the Wonderworker

Jesus never used his divine powers simply to amaze people and draw attention to himself. He used them instead to demonstrate God's compassion for people and his determination to save them through his Son.

The recorded stories -- of his changing water into wine, multiplying loaves and fishes, walking on the water, identifying the place of fish in the sea, calming a storm, withering a fig tree and his own glorious resurrection -- illustrate these truths.

"There was a wedding feast at Cana in Galilee. The mother of Jesus was there and Jesus and his disciples had also been invited. When they ran out of wine ... the mother of Jesus said to him, 'They have no wine.' ... Jesus said to the servants, 'Fill the jars with water ... draw some out now and take it to the steward.' They did this. The steward tasted the water and it had turned into wine. Having no idea where it came from...the steward called the bridegroom and said, 'People generally serve the best wine first ... but you have kept the best wine till now.' " (Jn 2:1-10).

Apparently there were two occasions when Jesus was moved by pity to multiply loaves and fishes to assuage the hunger of the great crowds which had followed him spellbound into some remote area. On the first occasion, which is recorded by Matthew, Mark, Luke and John, Jesus multiplied five loaves and two fish to feed five thousand men. (Women and children were not counted) Twelve baskets of leftovers were also gathered (Mt 14:13-21, Mk 6: 30-44, Lk 9:12-17, Jn 6:5-15).

The second miracle of compassion is recorded only by Matthew and Mark. Here Jesus multiplied seven loaves and a few fish to feed four-thousand men. (Women and children are still not numbered). Seven baskets of scraps were collected (Mt 15:32-38, Mk 8:1-10).

"Directly after this (the first multiplication of loaves and fishes) Jesus made his disciples get into the boat and go on ahead to Bethsaida, while he himself sent the crowd away ... When evening came, the boat was far out on the lake and he was alone on the land. He could see they were worn out with rowing, for the wind was against them. About the fourth watch of the night he came toward them, walking on the lake ... When they saw him walking on the lake they thought it was a ghost and cried out; for they had all seen him and were terrified. But he at once spoke to them and said, 'Courage! It is I! Do not be afraid!' Then he got into the boat with them and the wind dropped. They were utterly and completely dumbfounded, because they had not understood what the miracle of the loaves meant. Their minds were closed" (Mk 6:45-52, Mt 14:22-33, Jn 6:16-21).

"He got into one of the boats--it was Simon's--and asked him to put out a little from the shore. Then he sat down and taught the crowds from the boat. When he had finished speaking he said to Simon, 'Put out into deep water and pay out your nets for a catch.' 'Master,' Simon replied, 'We worked hard all night long and caught nothing, but if you say so, I will pay out the nets.' When they had done this they netted such a large number of fish that their nets began to tear. So they signaled to their companions in the other boat to come and help them. When these came, they filled the two boats to sinking point" (Lk 5:1-11).

In order to seek respite from the crowds, Jesus got into a boat with his disciples and sailed out into the Lake of Galilee. "Without warning a storm broke over the lake, so violent that the waves were breaking right over the boat. But Jesus was asleep. So they went to him and woke him saying: 'Save us, Lord, we are going down!' And he said to them, 'Why are you so frightened, you men of little faith?' With that he stood up and rebuked the winds and the sea and all was calm again. The men were astounded and said, 'Whatever kind of man is

86

this? Even the winds and the sea obey him.' " (Mt 8:23-27, Lk 8:22-25).

God requests only one thing of those who seek his help: that we have unwavering faith in his goodness and power. The story of the fig tree brings home this truth. "As he was returning to the city in the early morning, Jesus felt hungry. Seeing a fig tree by the road, he went up to it and found nothing on it but leaves. He said to it, 'May you never bear fruit again.' At that instant the fig tree withered. The disciples were amazed when they saw it ... Jesus answered, 'I tell you solemnly, if you have faith and do not doubt at all, not only will you do what I have done to the fig tree, but even if you say to this mountain, Get up and throw yourself into the sea, it will be done. If you have faith, everything you ask for in prayer you will receive.' " (Mt 21:18-22, Mk 11:12-14, 20-25).

Faith in the resurrection of Jesus forms the foundation of all Christian belief. As St. Paul said: "If Christ has not been raised then our preaching is useless and your believing is useless" (1 Cor 15:14). Once we receive the grace to believe in the resurrection of Jesus, then we are enabled to believe in his power to save us from sin and death. This is really the whole point. Christ rose bodily from the dead for *our* benefit, not his. The faith stories of the resurrection of Christ, which all the evangelists tell, were inspired by the Holy Spirit to help nourish our faith in the goodness and power of Jesus to save (Mt 28, Mk 16, Lk 24, Jn 20-21).

Jesus the Prophet

As we meditate upon the Gospels, particularly on the Gospel of John, we are impressed by the foreknowledge of Jesus. He did not alter his mind or plans because of events, especially the unpleasant ones. Jesus used events to accomplish his Father's purposes. This does not mean that the Father revealed every detail to the human mind of his Son. But it seems that Jesus knew from his earliest years why he had become a man and how he was going to accomplish the salvation of

87

every human being.

The Father also gave him insights into the teachings of the law and the prophets, which he revealed to others, captivating their minds and hearts. When he began his public ministry of preaching, the people quickly dubbed him: the prophet from Nazareth. "When he entered Jerusalem, the whole city was in turmoil. 'Who is this?' the people asked. And the crowds answered, 'This is the prophet, Jesus, from Nazareth in Galilee.' " (Mt 21:10-11).

At times the Father also enabled him to look into the hearts and minds of people, especially when they needed some special enlightment or correction. "Jesus never needed evidence about any man; he could tell what a man had in him" (Jn 2:25).

Accordingly we find many stories of conflict between Jesus and the official teachers (scribes, lawyers and Pharisees) in the Gospels. Jesus confronted their hidden hypocrisy, hoping to save them. Moreover, he forewarned Peter of his fall, and also let Judas know that he suspected his plans.

A prophet in the Old Testament was principally a spokesman, but also, at times, a seer. The Gospel stories show that Jesus fulfilled both aspects of the title.

In Matthew, Mark and Luke, Jesus made three predictions of his passion, death and resurrection. In John only one prediction is given.

The first prediction: Mt 15:21, Mk 8:31, Lk 9:22, Jn 12:23-35.
The second prediction: Mt 17:22, Mk 9:31, Lk 9:44.
The third prediction: Mt 20:17-20, Mk 10:32-34, Lk 18:31-34.

Matthew, Mark and Luke also relate Christ's prediction of the destruction of Jerusalem and the end of the world as we know it. (Mt 24, Mk 13, Lk 21:5-36)

All four evangelists give us the predictions of Peter's denials and

Judas' treachery (Mt 26:20-25,30-35, Mk 14:17-21,26-31, Lk 22:21-23,31-34, Jn 13:21-30,36-38).

Jesus the Servant

Greatness, in God's eyes, is achieved through service to others. This view has never been popular and is still not popular. Few people glory in the title of servant. Most people long to amass riches, so that they can hire others to do their menial work. Those who are hired by others look forward to the day when they can own their own business and make their own decisions. The majority of people desire to be liberated from accountability to others, which is expected of a servant or hired hand.

However, all the prophets understood this truth. They accepted their role of servant of Yahweh and of his people, even though the role often entailed misunderstandings, criticisms, complaints, rejection, suffering and even death at the hands of the people they were sent to serve.

The writer to the Hebrews points out that Jesus also understood this role and accepted it gladly. "Bulls' blood and goats' blood are useless for taking away sins. This is what he (Jesus) said, on coming into the world: 'You who wanted no sacrifice or oblation, prepared a body for me. You took no pleasure in holocausts or sacrifices for sin.' Then I said, just as I was commanded in the scroll of the book: 'God, here I am! I am coming to obey your will.' " (Heb 10:4-7).

Our Lord conveyed this message to those who wished to become his followers, but they were slow to accept it. They gloried in being associated with Jesus in his greatness. They looked forward to becoming chiefs, bosses, leaders who told others what to do.

"When the other ten (apostles) heard this (that James and John wanted the top positions in the kingdom) they were indignant with the two brothers. Jesus called them to him and said: 'You know that among the pagans the rulers lord it over them, and their great men

89

make their authority felt. This is not to happen among you. No. Anyone who wants to be great among you must be your servant; and anyone who wants to be first among you must be your slave, just as the Son of Man came not to be served but to serve and to give his life as a ransom for many.' " (Mt 20:20-28, Lk 22:24-27).

To bring home this truth dramatically, Christ donned a towel, poured water in a basin and began to wash the feet of his apostles on the night before he died. This was a duty normally reserved for slaves. When Peter objected, Jesus told him it was absolutely necessary. Unless Peter accepted the service and the lesson, he could not remain. The text then reads: "When he had washed their feet and put on his clothes again he went back to the table. 'Do you understand,' he said, 'what I have done to you? You call me Master and Lord, and rightly; so I am. If I, then, the Lord and Master, have washed your feet, you should wash each other's feet. I have given you an example so that you may copy what I have done to you. I tell you most solemnly, no servant is greater than his master, no messenger is greater than the man who sent him. Now that you know this, happiness will be yours if you behave accordingly.' " (Jn 13:1-17).

Yet when Christ was taken into custody, tortured and nailed to a cross, his apostles fled and hid. We, who now glory in being named among his associates, have much to reflect on and much to learn from the experiences of our predecessors.

The Servant Songs of Second Isaiah find their fulfillment in Jesus. "Here is my servant whom I have chosen, my beloved, the favorite of my soul. I will endow him with my spirit and he will proclaim the true faith to the nations. He will not brawl or shout, nor will anyone hear his voice in the streets. He will not break the crushed reed, nor put out the smoldering wick, till he has led the truth to victory. In his name the nations will put their hope" (Is 42:1-4, Mt 12:15-21).

Jesus the Light

The idea of living in perpetual darkness fills every sane person with fear. To be blinded is something we all dread. Accordingly, we relish the light of the sun, moon and stars. We enjoy the light of fires and lamps, and the electric lights that illuminate our homes, cars, roads, cities and places of work.

However, a darkness of mind and spirit exists that is worse than physical blackness. Not to know our dignity, not to know our destiny, or the means of maintaining them, leaves the mind and spirit in darkness. It robs a person of happiness and hope. It opens the door to philosophies which plunge human beings into deeper darkness. It enables the physically strong and economically powerful to exploit others for their own purposes.

Jesus is the God-sent light to end this darkness. "In the beginning was the Word: the Word was with God and the Word was God. He was with God in the beginning. Through him all things came to be; not one thing had its being but through him. All that came to be had life in him and that life was the light of men, a light that shines in the dark, a light that darkness could not overpower" (Jn 1:1-5).

Jesus understood his role as a light and referred to himself in this image: "I am the light of the world. Anyone who follows me will not be walking in the dark. He will have the light of life" (Jn 8:12). "As long as I am in the world I am the light of the world" (Jn 9:5). "The light will be with you only a little longer now. Walk while you have the light or the dark will overtake you. He who walks in the dark does not know where he is going. While you still have the light, believe in the light and you will become sons of light" (Jn 12:35-36). "I, the light, have come into the world, so that whoever believes in me need not stay in the dark any more" (Jn 12:46).

Jesus the Water of Life

The link between water and life is well known. Every living thing on the earth depends on water. Without it life vanishes. When Jesus referred to himself as the living water--the water that gives life--he conveyed a powerful message. Through him God's life enters us and gives lasting value to all we do. Apart from him even our greatest deeds have no meaning beyond our present existence. Those who reject Christ may be physically alive, but they are spiritually dead, with no hope of eternal happiness with God beyond their stay on earth.

To the woman of Samaria who came to draw water at Jacob's well Jesus said, "If you only knew what God is offering and who it is that is saying to you: Give me a drink, you would been the one to ask. And he would have given you living water. Whoever drinks this water (well water) will get thirsty again. Anyone who drinks the water that I shall give will never be thirsty again. The water that I shall give will turn into a spring inside him, welling up to eternal life" (Jn 4:10-13).

To the Jews he said: "He who believes in me will never thirst" (Jn 6:35). Christ alone satisfies our longing for meaning.

To the crowds at festival time he cried out, "If any man is thirsty, let him come to me! Let the man come and drink who believes in me!" John then added: "As scripture says: From his breast shall flow fountains of living water" (Jn 7:37-38). These words harken back to the prophecy of Ezekiel (Ez 47) which spoke of waters flowing out from the temple, bringing life to everything they touch.

In the Catholic Church the words of Christ and Ezekiel have always been linked to the sacrament of baptism, through which, with the other sacraments, our spirits receive God's life. This source of life was manifested when blood and water flowed from Christ's pierced side as he hung on the cross.

Jesus the Bread of Life

Bread has been the staple food of most people for thousands of years. It has become one of the chief symbols of life, because when bread is abundant, life prospers; when bread is scarce, life is in jeopardy.

Our spirits need nourishment, just like our bodies. What we feed them determines their health and vigor. Accordingly, Jesus referred to himself as the bread of life, because he gives faith, hope and the ability to love--the basics which our souls crave. He is "the bread come down from heaven" which the Father sends to nourish us on our pilgrimage. If we eat this bread we will remain strong, be able to help others, and finish our journey full of vigor. If we refuse to eat this bread, we will grow weaker and weaker, unable to assist others, and will finally die before we reach our final destination.

To the Jews Jesus said, "I tell you most solemnly, it was not Moses who gave you bread from heaven. It is my Father who gives you the bread from heaven, the true bread; for the bread of God is that which comes down from heaven and gives life to the world ... I am the bread of life. He who comes to me will never be hungry ... Your fathers ate the manna in the desert and they are dead. But this is the bread that comes down from heaven. Anyone who eats this bread will live forever. And the bread that I give is my flesh for the life of the world" (Jn 6:32-51).

When they started to argue over his statements, Jesus added, "I tell you most solemnly, if you do not eat the flesh of the Son of Man and drink his blood, you will not have life in you. Anyone who eats my flesh and drinks my blood has eternal life and I shall raise him up on the last day. For my flesh is real food and my blood is real drink. He who eats my flesh and drinks my blood lives in me and I live in him. As I, who am sent by the living Father, myself draw life from the Father, so whoever eats me will draw life from me. This is the bread come down from heaven; not like the bread our ancestors ate; they are dead, but anyone who eats this bread will live forever" (Jn 6:53-58).

93

Just how the words were to be realized, Jesus later revealed. On the night before he died, while he was celebrating the Paschal Feast with his disciples: "Jesus took some bread and when he had said the blessing he broke it and gave it to the disciples. 'Take it and eat,' he said, 'this is my body.' Then he took a cup, and when he had returned thanks he gave it to them. 'Drink all of you from this,' he said, 'for this is my blood, the blood of the covenant, which is to be poured out for many for the forgiveness of sins.' " (Mt 26:26-29, Mk 14:22-25, Lk 22:19-20).

We who believe in Christ are nourished not only by his words, but also by his body and blood which we receive under the forms of bread and wine. When we receive the sacraments, especially the Eucharist, Christ gives us the strength we need to live according to his teachings.

Jesus the Road to Life

Today we travel often, sometimes to far away places. We know how important maps and signs are to arrive at our destination. A wrong turn can mean lots of time and gasoline lost. So it is essential that we study our maps carefully before setting out and that we pay attention to signs, so that we will get on the right road and stay on it.

Our final destination in life is eternal union with the wonderful God who made us and loves us so much that he sent his own Son to guide us along the way. Jesus is the road back to the Father. As long as we pay attention to him and travel with him, we will reach our final end happily. To ignore him, to leave him, always spells disaster. We could get lost forever.

To Thomas, the apostle, Jesus said, " 'I am going now to prepare a place for you, and after I have gone and prepared you a place, I shall return to take you with me, so that where I am, you may be too. You know the way to the place where I am going.' Thomas said, 'Lord we do not know where you are going, so how can we know the way?'

94

Jesus said: 'I am the Way, the Truth and the Life. No one can come to the Father except through me.' " (Jn 14:2-6).

Jesus the Vine

Few people own grape vines today, yet we know that branches can bear fruit only as long as they remain attached to their trees and vines. So the truth that Jesus wished to convey by his image of the vine and branches is as valid today as it was 2,000 years ago. In union with Christ all our actions have meaning, no matter how insignificant they seem to others. Apart from him, they lose their meaning, no matter how grand they seem in the eyes of people. This truth has inspired countless men and women to live lives of quiet heroism and generosity, for they know that whatever they do in union with Christ, and out of love for Christ, he always remembers.

Interestingly, John used the image of Jesus the vine during the meal before his Passion. He did this to help believers grasp the importance of the Eucharist to their salvation. "I am the true vine and my Father is the vinedresser. Every branch in me that bears no fruit he cuts away and every branch that does bear fruit he prunes to make it bear even more ... I am the vine, you are the branches. Whoever remains in me, with me in him, bears fruit in plenty. Cut off from me you can do nothing. Anyone who does not remain in me is like a branch that has been thrown away; he withers. These branches are collected and thrown on the fire and they are burned ... It is to the glory of my Father that you should bear much fruit and then you will be my disciples" (Jn 15:1-8).

Jesus the Friend

Most of us have many acquaintances but few friends. A really good friend is, as says the Book of Ecclesiasticus: "a sure shelter, a rare treasure, beyond price, the elixir of life" (Sir 6:14-17).

When Jesus used the image of the vine, he spoke of himself as a friend among friends. "A man can have no greater love than to lay down his life for his friends. You are my friends if you do what I command you. I shall not call you servants any more, because a servant does not know his master's business; I call you friends, because I have made known to you everything I have learned from my Father. You did not choose me. No, I chose you" (Jn 15:13-15).

Jesus the Good Shepherd

Shepherds in our Lord's time were often drop-outs from society who took on the job of caring for sheep and goats as a means of staying alive. Some of them grew to love the animals. Others abused them and abandoned them at the least sign of danger. Jesus referred to himself as the Good Shepherd, a man who loved his charges and took good care of them, a man who was even willing to lay down his life to protect them from harm.

"Tell me. Suppose a man has a hundred sheep and one of them strays. Will he not leave the ninety-nine on the hillside and go in search of the stray? I tell you solemnly, if he finds it, it gives him more joy than do the ninety-nine that did not stray at all. Similarly, it is never the will of your Father in heaven that one of these little ones should be lost" (Mt 18:12-14).

"I am the good shepherd. I know my own and my own know me. Just as the Father knows me and I know the Father. And I lay down my life for my sheep. There are other sheep I have that are not of this fold and these I have to lead as well. They too will listen to my voice and there will be only one flock and one shepherd" (Jn 10:11-18).

Jesus referred to this imagery again when he entrusted the care of followers to Peter. "After the meal Jesus said to Simon Peter, 'Simon, son of John, do you love me more than these others do?' He answered, 'Yes, Lord, you know I love you.' Jesus said to him, 'Feed my lambs.' A second time he said to him, 'Simon, son of John, do you love me?' He replied, 'Yes, Lord, you know I love you.' Jesus said to him, 'Look after my sheep.' Then he said to him a third time,

'Simon, son of John, do you love me?' Peter was upset that he asked him the third time, 'Do you love me?' and said: 'Lord, you know everything; you know I love you.' Jesus said to him, 'Feed my sheep.' " (Jn 21:16-17).

Jesus the Mother Hen

Anyone who has ever watched a hen protect her brood immediately appreciates this image of concern which Jesus applied to himself. A hen will take on a much larger animal and endanger itself to protect her chicks from harm. What the hen does from instinct Jesus does freely and out of love for God's children.

"Jerusalem, Jerusalem, you that kill the prophets and stone those who are sent to you! How often have I longed to gather your children, as a hen gathers her chicks under her wings, and you refused! So be it! Your house will be left to you desolate, for I promise, you shall not see me any more until you say: 'Blessings on him who comes in the name of the Lord!' " (Mt 23:37-39).

Jesus the Bridegroom

The parable of the ten bridesmaids revives the imagery of the Song of Songs in which the bridegroom and bride exchange their feelings of love for each other. In this parable Jesus is the bridegroom who comes to celebrate eternally with his bride (the church) and all who love him. Those who are prepared, i.e. those who have remained faithful and obedient to God, are permitted to enter the wedding hall (heaven). The others are excluded from their joy and are locked outside in the darkness (Mt 25:1-13).

Jesus the King

Only in parables did Jesus refer to himself as a king, although he knew that he was the king promised of old to the Chosen People. His restraint was freely chosen in view of the people's expectation of an earthly monarch, a military warrior, who would liberate them from the oppression of the Romans. Indeed, he fled from those who sought to take him by force and declare him their political leader (cf. Jn 6:15).

While standing before the governor, Pilate, Jesus did not deny being a king. However, he clarified for Pilate the nature of his kingship. His kingdom was not of this world. He was the king of truth. All who love truth, listen to his voice and belong to his kingdom. These he rules and will reward when one day he returns to earth in all his glory and power.

"When the Son of Man comes in his glory ... all the nations will be assembled before him ... Then the king will say to those on his right hand, 'Come, you whom my Father has blessed, take for your heritage the kingdom prepared for you since the foundation of the world' ... Next he will say to those on his left hand, 'Go away from me ... to the eternal fire prepared for the devil and his angels...' " (Mt 25:31-46).

"The kingdom of heaven may be compared to a king who gave a feast for his son's wedding ... When the king came in to look at the guests he noticed one man who was not wearing a wedding garment and said to him, 'How did you get in here, my friend, without a wedding garment?'... Then the king said to the attendants, 'Bind him hand and foot and throw him out into the dark, where there will be weeping and grinding of teeth.' For many are called, but few are chosen" (Mt 22:1-14).

"Pilate went back into the Praetorium and called Jesus to him. 'Are you the king of the Jews?' he asked ... Jesus replied, 'Mine is not a kingdom of this world; if my kingdom were of this world, my men would have fought to prevent my being surrendered to the Jews. But my kingdom is not of this kind.' 'So, you are a king then?' said Pilate. 'It is you who say it,' answered Jesus. "Yes, I am a king. I was born for this. I came into the world for this to bear witness to the truth. All who are on the side of truth listen to my voice.' " (Jn 18:28-40).

"Pilate wrote out a notice and had it fixed to the cross. It ran: 'Jesus, the Nazarene, King of the Jews.' The notice was read by many of the Jews, because the place where Jesus was crucified was not far from the city and the writing was in Hebrew, Latin and Greek. So the Jewish chief priests said to Pilate, 'You should not write *King of the Jews, but This man said: I am the King of the Jews.*' Pilate answered, 'What I have written, I have written.' " (Jn 19:19-22).

Jesus the Father

Throughout his life Jesus referred to God as his Father. It therefore came as a shock to his apostle, Philip, when Jesus declared that he and the Father were one. He, the Father and the Spirit created all things and maintain them in being. He is in the Father and the Father is in him. All who are born of the Spirit are born of the Father and Son. All prayers directed to God are directed as well to the Father, Son and Holy Spirit. All parables about the Father apply not only to the Father, but also to the Son and Holy Spirit. We can, therefore, correctly call Jesus our Father, because he is the source of our life; he is our caretaker, guide and savior.

"Philip said, 'Lord, let us see the Father and then we shall be satisfied.' 'Have I been with you all this time, Philip,' said Jesus to him, 'and you still do not know me? To have seen me is to have seen the Father, so how can you say, Let us see the Father? Do you not believe that I am in the Father and the Father is in me? The words I say to you I do not speak as from myself. It is the Father, living in me, who is doing this work.' " (Jn 14:5-13).

"One of his disciples said, 'Lord, teach us to pray, just as John taught his disciples.' He said to them, 'Say, when you pray: Father, may your name be held holy, your kingdom come...' " (Lk 11:1-4, Mt 6:9-13).

To the Jews he said: "The sheep that belong to me listen to my voice ... The Father who gave them to me is greater than anyone and no one can steal from the Father. The Father and I are one ... If I am not

99

doing my Father's work, there is no need to believe me; but if I am doing it, then even if you refuse to believe in me, at least believe in the work I do; then you will know for sure that the Father is in me and I am in the Father" (Jn 10:22-38).

CHAPTER EIGHT

IMAGES OF GOD IN THE ACTS OF THE APOSTLES

A Second-Century tradition names St. Luke, author of the third Gospel, as the composer of the Acts as well. Biblical scholars confirm the styles of writing to be the same. So we can expect the Acts to reflect the predominant images of God in the Gospels: the Teacher, the Healer and the Wonderworker. In fact, this is what we find as we read the book.

Biblical scholars also tell us that Luke's purpose in writing Acts was to show that the Holy Spirit had enabled the first Christians to recognize themselves as the new People of God, a people commissioned to bring the message of salvation, through belief in Jesus, to all nations.

Luke wrote in the form of a religious travelogue in order to relay how this was accomplished. The main two characters of his work are Peter, the fisherman who denied knowing Christ, and Paul, who had persecuted Him. Yet Christ chose to touch the hearts of many people through the preaching of these two converted sinners. He healed many others through their prayers. He worked marvelous signs to confirm the authority he gave them.

Jesus the Teacher

It is awesome to realize that God chose ordinary human beings to continue the work of his beloved Son. The realization of this truth must have frightened the first followers of Christ. Yet as soon as the apostles and disciples received the Holy Spirit from Jesus, they assumed with confidence his ministry of teaching, healing and sanctifying. The Spirit enabled them to realize that Jesus was teaching, healing and sanctifying through them. Their own shortcomings, weaknesses, even sins did not dismay them, because they knew that Christ, the Sinless One, was illuminating minds,

101

converting wills, and healing hearts. Of course, they tried to imitate, as far as possible, the holiness of their Master, but they knew that Christ would supplement their shortcomings and forgive their failings. This conviction persists in the church, as she strives to help others know, love and follow Christ.

During the meal before his Passion Jesus told his followers that he would send the Spirit of Truth to clarify all things for them and to enable them to witness before all people (Jn 14).

Luke opens the Acts with all the disciples waiting for their new Advocate, while they recalled the promise of Jesus: "You will receive power when the Holy Spirit comes on you and then you will be my witnesses not only in Jerusalem but throughout Judea and Samaria and indeed to the ends of the earth" (Acts 1:8).

When the Spirit came, in the form of a powerful wind and tongues of fire, they emerged fearless from seclusion and began to teach those who had been drawn to their dwelling by the noise. Peter addressed those who had gathered: "God has raised this man Jesus to life and all of us are witnesses to that ... Israel can be certain that God has made this Jesus whom you crucified both Lord and Christ ... He spoke to them for a long time using many arguments and urged them: 'Save yourselves from this perverse generation.' They were convinced by his arguments and accepted what he said and were baptized. That very day about three thousand were added to their number" (Acts 2:1-41).

When a lame man was cured by Peter's invocation of Jesus, he used the occasion to instruct the amazed people about the meaning of Jesus' life, death and resurrection. He encouraged them to repent and believe in Christ. "Now I know, brothers, that neither you nor your leaders had any idea what you were really doing ... Now you must repent and turn to God, so that your sins may be wiped out and so that the Lord may send the time of comfort" (Acts 3).

Filled with the Holy Spirit, Peter did not hesitate to teach the Council of Jewish leaders (Sanhedrin) about the salvation wrought through Jesus. "If you are questioning us today about an act of kindness to a cripple, and asking us how he was healed, then I am glad to tell you all ... that it was by the name of Jesus Christ the Nazarene, the one you crucified, whom God raised from the dead, by this name and by no other that this man is able to stand up perfectly healthy, here in your presence today" (Acts 4).

When he and the other apostles were again arraigned before the Sanhedrin, he repeated his instructions. "It was the God of our ancestors who raised up Jesus, but it was you who had him executed by hanging on a tree. By his own right hand God has raised him up to be leader and savior, to give repentance and forgiveness of sins through him to Israel" (Acts 5).

Stephen, the Deacon, fearlessly reviewed God's kindness toward Israel before the Sanhedrin, while pointing out the history of their stubbornness toward him. "You who had the Law brought to you by angels are the very ones who have not kept it" (Acts 7).

Peter corrected Simon, the magician, who thought he could purchase the powers of the Holy Spirit with money. "You have no share, no right, in this. God can see how your heart is warped. Repent of this wickedness of yours and pray to the Lord. You may still be forgiven for thinking as you did" (Acts 8:9-25).

Philip, the Deacon, enlightened the Ethiopian eunuch about Jesus, beginning with the text of Isaiah. "Starting with this text of scripture, Philip proceeded to explain the Good News of Jesus to him" (Acts 8:26-40).

After his conversion Paul began immediately to preach about Jesus. "After he had spent only a few days with the disciples in Damascus, Paul began preaching in the synagogues, 'Jesus is the Son of God.' ... When he got to Jerusalem he preached fearlessly in the name of the

103

Lord" (Acts 9:1-25).

After Peter learned from the Holy Spirit in a vision that all foods and people are clean, he conveyed this message to the Roman centurion, Cornelius. "The truth I have now come to realize, Peter said, is that God does not have favorites, but that anybody of any nationality who fears God and does what is right is acceptable to him ... Jesus Christ is Lord of all people ... God has ordered us to proclaim that he has appointed him to judge everyone, alive or dead. It is to him that all the prophets bear this witness: that all who believe in Jesus will have their sins forgiven through his name" (Acts 10).

When they met in Jerusalem, Peter taught the other apostles this truth and also their duty to preach to all peoples. "I realized then that God was giving them (the pagans) the identical thing he gave to us when we believed in the Lord Jesus Christ; and who was I to stand in God's way?" (Acts 11:1-18).

Barnabas taught the Good News of the Lord Jesus in Antioch. "And a large number of people were won over to the Lord ... It was at Antioch that the disciples were first called: Christians" (Acts 11:19-26).

Paul and Barnabas traveled through many cities and towns of Asia Minor preaching about Christ and explaining the meaning of the scriptures to Jews and Gentiles alike. "My brothers, I want you to realize that it is through Jesus that forgiveness of your sins is proclaimed. Through him justification from all sins, which the Law of Moses was unable to justify, is offered to every believer" (Acts 13:38-39).

"We had to proclaim the word of God to you first, but since you have rejected it ... we must turn to the pagans ... It made the pagans very happy to hear this and they thanked the Lord for his message: all who were destined for eternal life became believers" (Acts 13:46-49).

Paul corrected the misunderstanding of the pagans, who thought that he and Barnabas were gods because they had cured a cripple through the power of Jesus. "We have come with good news to make you turn from these empty idols to the living God who made heaven and earth and the sea and all that these hold" (Acts 14:8-18).

Peter clarified for the apostles and disciples their freedom from the customs and traditions of the Law. "It would only provoke God's anger now, surely, if you imposed on the disciples the very burden that neither we nor our ancestors were strong enough to support" (Acts 15:1-12).

James pointed out to the Jewish Christians the need to avoid scandal in following their new-found freedom. "Instead of making things more difficult for pagans who turn to God, send them a letter telling them merely to abstain from anything polluted by idols, from fornication, from the meat of strangled animals and from blood. For Moses has always had his preachers in every town and is read aloud in the synagogues every sabbath" (Acts 15:13-21).

Silas, Timothy and Luke joined Paul in his preaching in Asia Minor. Lydia, a dye worker, was converted. "She listened to us and the Lord opened her heart to accept what Paul was saying. After she and her household had been baptized she sent us an invitation: 'Come and stay with us.' " (Acts 16:11-15).

During their imprisonment in Philippi, Paul and Silas converted their jailer. "They preached the word of the Lord to him and to all his family. Late as it was, he took them to wash their wounds and was baptized then and there with all his household. Afterward he took them home and gave them a meal, and the whole family celebrated their conversion to belief in God" (Acts 16:25-40).

Paul convinced some of the Jews in Thessalonika that Jesus was the Holy One referred to in the Scriptures. "And the Christ," he said, "is this Jesus whom I am proclaiming to you." Some of them were convinced and joined Paul and Silas and so did a great many God-fearing people and Greeks, as well as a number of rich women (Acts 17:1-4).

The people of Beroea readily welcomed the missionaries. "Here the Jews were more open-minded than those in Thessalonika. They welcomed the word very readily. Every day they studied the scriptures to check whether it was true. Many Jews became believers and so did many Greek women from the upper classes and a number of the men" (Acts 17:10-15).

Paul confronted the philosophers and cynics of Athens who scoffed at the notion of a future life. "Since we are the children of God, we have no excuse for thinking that the deity looks like anything in gold, silver or stone that has been carved and designed by a man. God has overlooked that sort of thing when men were ignorant, but now he is telling everyone everywhere that they must repent, because he has fixed a day when the whole world will be judged and judged in righteousness. And he has appointed a man to be the judge. God has publicly proved this by raising this man from the dead" (Acts 17: 16-31).

In Corinth Paul's preaching converted the president of the synagogue and a great many others too. "Crispus, president of the synagogue, and his whole household became believers in the Lord. A great many Corinthians who had heard him became believers and were baptized" (Acts 18:5-9).

In Ephesus, Priscilla and Aquila instructed the learned preacher, Apollos. After his conversion, he became an energetic exponent of Christ. "When Priscilla and Aquila heard Apollos speak boldly in the synagogue, they took an interest in him and gave him further instruction about the Way" (Acts 18:24-28).

While in Ephesus, Paul also enlightened twelve of John the Baptist's disciples, who converted to Christ. "John insisted that the people should believe in the one who was to come after him--in other words, Jesus. When they heard this, they were baptized in the name of the Lord Jesus" (Acts 19:1-7).

When brought before the Sanhedrin in Jerusalem for trial, Paul did not hesitate to proclaim to them, "It is for our hope in the resurrection of the dead that I am on trial" (Acts 23:1-11).

Paul repeated his message before the Roman governor, Felix: "It is according to the Way, which they describe as a sect, that I worship the God of my ancestors, retaining my belief in all points of the Law and in what is written in the prophets; and I hold the same hope in God as they do that there will be a resurrection of good men and bad men alike" (Acts 24:1-21).

After two years of imprisonment in Caesarea, Paul repeated his message again to King Agrippa, his wife, his notables and all the Jewish leaders: "I was blessed with God's help and so I have stood firm to this day, testifying to great and small alike, saying nothing more than what the prophets and Moses himself said would happen: that the Christ was to suffer and that, as the first to rise from the dead, he was to proclaim that light now shone for our people and for the pagans too" (Acts 25-26).

During his final years of imprisonment in Rome Paul never ceased carrying out his mission: "He welcomed all who came to visit him, proclaiming the kingdom of God and teaching the truth about the Lord Jesus Christ with complete freedom and without hindrance from anyone" (Acts 28:30-31).

Jesus the Healer

Through the enlightenment of the Holy Spirit, Christians believed that Christ was with them in a real, but hidden way. They believed that he spoke through them as they expounded the Scriptures. They also did not hesitate to call upon him to heal those afflicted in mind or

107

body. The healings that are recorded in the Acts were occasions for great rejoicing. Each cure confirmed that Jesus was with them, and that he would remain with them to the end of time.

Prior to relating the cure of a lame man, Luke mentions that the apostles had worked many miracles and signs that impressed everyone (Acts 2:43). He also describes the great transformation of heart that had taken place among believers in Christ. This change (cure?) was so startling that it drew the attention of everyone. "The faithful all lived together and owned everything in common. They sold their goods and possessions and shared out the proceeds among themselves according to what each one needed. They went as a body to the Temple every day, but met in their houses for the breaking of the bread. They shared their food gladly and generously. They praised God and were looked up to by everyone" (Acts 2:42-47).

The cure of the Temple beggar, who had been crippled from birth, astonished everyone who knew him. As he leapt about and praised God for his mercy, he told everyone how he had looked to Peter and John for alms and heard these words from Peter: "I have neither silver nor gold, but I will give you what I have. In the name of Jesus Christ the Nazarene, walk!" From that moment he felt his feet and ankles become firm and the urge to rise surge through his legs. Jesus, the Nazarene, had cured him! (Acts 3:1-10).

Although the general populace admired the followers of Christ, many failed to join them openly for fear of being excluded from worship in the synagogue. But the many cures affected by the apostles held them spellbound. "So many signs and wonders were worked among the people at the hands of the apostles that the sick were even taken out into the streets and laid on beds and sleeping mats in the hope that at least the shadow of Peter might fall across some of them as he went past. People even came crowding in from the towns around about Jerusalem, bringing with them their sick and those tormented by unclean spirits and all of them were cured" (Acts 5:12-16).

When their arch-persecutor, Saul, was blinded on his way to Damascus, God sent Ananias to cure him. "He entered the house and at once laid his hands on Saul and said, 'Brother Saul, I have been sent by the Lord Jesus who appeared to you on your way here so that you may recover your sight and be filled with the Holy Spirit.' Immediately it was as though scales fell away from Saul's eyes and he could see again." The healed persecutor proceeded to become the foremost missionary of the early church (Acts 9).

While visiting the people of Lydda, Peter cured a paralytic who had been bedridden for eight years. "Peter said to him, 'Aeneas, Jesus Christ cures you. Get up and fold up your sleeping mat.' Aeneas got up immediately; everybody who lived in Lydda and Sharon saw him and they were all converted to the Lord" (Acts 9:32-25).

When he came to the town of Jaffa, the widows told Peter about Tabitha, a woman of great charity who had recently died. Moved by their tears he visited the room where she was laid out and prayed. Then he said: "Tabitha, stand up." She opened her eyes, looked at Peter and sat up. Peter helped her to her feet. Then he called in the disciples and widows and showed them she was alive. The whole of Jaffa heard about it and many believed in the Lord" (Acts 9:36-42).

In Lystra Paul saw a man who had suffered from crippled feet since birth. Sensing his faith in Christ he said in a loud voice: "'Get to your feet; stand up!' And the cripple jumped up and began to walk" (Acts 14:8-18).

In Philippi Paul commanded an evil spirit to vacate a woman it had possessed. "'I order you in the name of Jesus Christ to leave that woman.' The spirit went out of her, then and there" (Acts 16:16-24).

In Ephesus Paul brought back to life a young man who had fallen three stories to the ground. "A young man called Eutychus who was sitting on the windowsill grew drowsy and was overcome by sleep and fell to the ground three floors below. He was picked up dead.

Paul went down and stooped to clasp the boy to him. 'There is no need to worry,' he said, 'there is still life in him.' Then he went back upstairs where he broke bread and ate and carried on talking till he left at daybreak. They took the boy away alive and were greatly encouraged" (Acts 20:7-12).

In Malta Paul cured the father of the prefect, Publius, and many others. "It so happened that Publius' father was in bed, suffering from feverish attacks and dysentery. Paul went in to see him, and after a prayer he laid his hands on the man and healed him. When this happened, the other sick people on the island came as well and were cured" (Acts 28:7-10).

Jesus the Wonderworker

Luke tells us that besides the many cures which Jesus worked through his apostles, he also effected other signs and wonders. Apparently he did this to confirm the prophetic teaching of his apostles.

The first wonder which Luke relates concerns the sudden death of a couple who sought to deceive the community by falsifying the amount given from the sale of their property. "Peter said, 'So you and your husband have agreed to put the Spirit of the Lord to the test! What made you do it? You hear those footsteps? They have just been to bury your husband; they will carry you out too.' Instantly she dropped dead at his feet. When the young men came in they found she was dead. They carried her out and buried her by the side of her husband. This made a profound impression on the whole church and on all who heard it" (Acts 5:1-11).

The second wonder occurred when a messenger from God liberated the apostles from jail. "Prompted by jealousy, they (the Sadducees) arrested the apostles and had them put in the common jail. But at night the angel of the Lord opened the prison gates and said as he led them out, 'Go stand in the Temple and tell the people all about this new Life.' " (Acts 5:17-21).

Another liberation story is related in chapter twelve: this time Herod had jailed Peter, in order to please the Jewish leaders. During the night, while Peter slept chained between two soldiers, he heard a voice: "'Hurry!' And the chains fell from his hands. 'Put on your belt and sandals ... wrap your cloak around you and follow me.' Peter followed the angel, but ... thought he was seeing a vision. They passed through two guard posts one after the other and reached the iron gate leading to the city. This opened of its own accord. They went through it and had walked the whole length of one street when suddenly the angel left him. It was only then that Peter came to himself. 'Now I know it is all true,' he said" (Acts 12:1-19).

When the magician, Elymas, tried to prevent the proconsul Sergius of Paulus' conversion to Christ, Paul asked Christ to punish the man. "'Why don't you stop twisting the straightforward ways of the Lord? Now watch how the hand of the Lord will strike you. You will be blind and for a time you will not see the sun.' That instant, everything went misty and dark for him and he groped about to find someone to lead him by the hand. The proconsul, who had watched everything, became a believer, being astonished by what he had learned about the Lord" (Acts 13:4-12).

A third prison liberation story is recorded in chapter sixteen. Paul and Silas had been flogged and thrown into the prison of Philippi. "Late that night Paul and Silas were praying and singing God's praises, while the other prisoners listened. Suddenly there was an earthquake that shook the prison to its foundations. All the doors flew open and the chains fell from all the prisoners" (Acts 16:16-40).

The final liberation story took place on the isle of Malta, where the survivors of the shipwreck were warming themselves around a fire. "Paul had collected a bundle of sticks and was putting them on the fire, when a viper brought out by the heat attached itself to his hand. When the natives saw the creature hanging from his hand, they said to one another, 'That man must be a murderer; he may have escaped

111

the sea, but divine vengeance would not let him live.' However, Paul shook the creature off into the fire and came to no harm, although they were expecting him at any moment to swell up or drop dead on the spot. After they had waited a long time without seeing anything out of the ordinary happen to him, they changed their minds and began to say he was a god" (Acts 28:1-6).

CHAPTER NINE

IMAGES OF GOD IN THE LETTERS OF PAUL

Thirteen letters are attributed to the apostle Paul, all of which deepen our understanding of God and of his Son, Jesus. The letters, which were written over a twenty-year period, offer profound insights on the rest of Scripture. They also shed light on the unique relationship that now exists between believers and Jesus. In a real, but mysterious, way Christ continues to live, grow, work, teach, heal, suffer, die and rise in his members. What believers do, Christ does. What we do to one another, we do to Christ.

The Holy Spirit initiated these insights in Paul when he caused him to reflect upon the words which he heard from the heavens on his way to Damascus, on his way to capture and imprison all followers of Christ: "Saul, Saul, why are you persecuting me? ... I am Jesus, and you are persecuting me" (Acts 9:4-5).

"It was by a revelation that I was given the knowledge of the mystery ... the mystery of Christ ... unknown to men in past generations ... It means that the pagans now share the same inheritance (as Jews), that they are parts of the same body and that the promise has been made to them in Christ Jesus, through the Gospel (the preaching of the Good News)" (Eph 3:3-7).

Paul came to realize that the union of believers with Christ is different from other human associations. Once the union is formed it lasts forever. Whatever believers do, good or bad, affects Christ and his here-and-now ability to touch the minds and hearts of believers and non-believers alike. Whatever believers do also affects the extension of Christ's kingdom, furthering or delaying it.

These insights dominated Paul's thoughts and preaching. They enabled him to work indefatigably and to suffer joyfully the many hardships that came his way. That is why he could say with

113

conviction to the Colossians, "It makes me happy to suffer for you, as I am suffering now, and in my own body to do what I can to make up for all that has still to be undergone by Christ for the sake of his body, the church" (Col 1:24).

Our understanding of the church as "the Body of Christ" originated with Paul. To his way of thinking, Christians truly represented Christ to the world. Therefore they had to strive after holiness. In his first letter to the Corinthians he reminded them of this truth: "You know, surely, that your bodies are members making up the body of Christ ... Keep away from fornication ... Your body, you know, is the temple of the Holy Spirit, who is in you since you received him from God. You are not your own property. You have been bought and paid for. That is why you should use your body for the glory of God" (1 Cor 6:12-20).

Paul encouraged all the baptized to have the same mind as Christ. The Holy Spirit would help them, if they asked him. Christ would "take over" their lives, if they permitted him. To the extent that they permitted him, Christ would extend his saving mission of teaching, healing, sanctifying all people on earth. In the words of Paul: "We, with our unveiled faces reflecting like mirrors the brightness of the Lord, all grow brighter and brighter as we are turned into the image that we reflect. This is the work of the Lord who is spirit" (2 Cor 3:18).

This exciting concept of Paul's has stimulated Christians through the ages and continues to do so today. Those who live it realize how it transforms the mind and heart. It brings a fresh, new view to everything and every person. It strengthens the weak and timid, enabling them to persevere in goodness under trial. It encourages boldness for the sake of the kingdom and patience in the face of difficulties. It fills every waking moment of the faithful with joy, as they await their face-to-face meeting with the One whom they love and serve.

Jesus the Teacher

Jesus continues to instruct Christians through the writings of his servant, Paul. I've highlighted the themes which Christ teaches through Paul's letters, in order to encourage appreciation of our Christian calling, its dignity and power to change the world.

If we are to fully appreciate Paul's messages, we need to grasp his fundamental view of Christ, of himself and of all Christians: all were servants, servants of God and servants of others. This basic outlook permeates all his letters and challenges our personal philosophy of life.

PAULINE THEME ONE: CHRISTIAN SERVANTS

"We have received the Spirit that comes from God, to teach us to understand the gifts that he has given us. Therefore we teach, not in the way in which philosophy is taught, but in the way the Spirit teaches us" (1 Cor 2:12).

Philosophers in Paul's time taught that the purpose of life was the acquisition of knowledge. Knowledge gave a person power. The knowledgeable person was able to control his own destiny, the minds of others and even the world about him. Knowledge made a person a master of himself and others. Such a view ignored the power of wayward passions. However, it filled a person with unwarranted pride, inclining him to look down on those who did not have the same degree of knowledge. It also contained the seeds of injustice, for it permitted exploitation of others in the cause of learning. The Spirit, on the other hand, brought knowledge of total dependence on God and a call to respect and serve others. "Knowledge gives self-importance; it is love that makes the building grow" (1 Cor 8:1).

This attitude was critical for Paul. It was the attitude of Christ himself: "His state was divine; yet he did not cling to his equality with God, but emptied himself to assume the condition of a slave and became as men are. And being as all men are, he was humbler yet, even to accepting death, death on a cross" (Col 2:6-7). Paul characterized himself as a servant. He rejoiced when other Christians understood their role as servants, and he admonished those who seemed to adopt a different role.

While Paul began every one of his letters by reminding his readers of his position as apostle, on several occasions he gloried in his title of servant: "From Paul, a servant of Christ Jesus who has been called to be an apostle ..." (Rom 1:1). "From Paul and Timothy, servants of Christ Jesus ..." (Phil 1:1). "From Paul, servant of God, an apostle of Jesus Christ ..." (Ti 1:1).

Paul's view of himself as a servant also reappears throughout his letters: "People must think of us as Christ's servants, stewards entrusted with the mysteries of God. What is expected of stewards is that each one should be found worthy of his trust" (1 Cor 4:1-2). "It is not ourselves that we are preaching, but Christ Jesus as the Lord, and ourselves as servants for Jesus' sake" (2 Cor 4:6). "We do nothing that people might object to, so as not to bring discredit on our function as God's servants. Instead, we prove ourselves as servants of God by great fortitude in times of suffering, in time of hardship and distress ..." (2 Cor 6:3-10). "I have been made the servant of that gospel by a gift of grace from God who gave it to me by his own power" (Eph 3:7).

Paul also rejoiced when the Thessalonians grasped this view: "We know, brothers, that God loves you ... because when we brought the Good News to you, it came to you not only as words, but as power ... as utter conviction ... and you became imitators of us and of the Lord ... this has made you the example to all believers in Macedonia and Achaia ... when you were converted to God and became servants of the real, living God ..." (1 Thes 1:4-10). "A servant of the Lord is not to engage in quarrels, but has to be kind to everyone, a good teacher and patient" (2 Tm 2:24).

116

PAULINE THEME TWO: CHRISTIAN DIGNITY

While Paul wanted Christians to look upon themselves as servants, servants of Christ and of their fellow human beings, he also desired that they should frequently recall the dignity which God had freely given them, so as not to lose heart:

"You are God's chosen race, his saints. He loves you" (Col 3:12).

"You are all sons of light and sons of the day; we do not belong to the night or to darkness" (1 Thes 5:5).

"Realize that you are God's temple and that the Spirit of God was living among you" (1 Cor 3:16-17).

"We are ambassadors for Christ. It is as though God were appealing through us. And the appeal that we make in Christ's name is: Be reconciled to God" (2 Cor 5:20).

"The Spirit himself and our spirit bear united witness that we are children of God. And if we are children, we are heirs as well: heirs of God and co-heirs with Christ, sharing his suffering so as to share his glory" (Rom 8:17).

"Not all the descendants of Abraham are his true children ... it is only the children of the promise who will count as true descendants" (Rom 9:7-8).

"Before the world was made, God chose us, ... to be for his greater glory, the people who would put their hopes in Christ ..." (Eph 1:4-14).

"You are no longer aliens or foreign visitors. You are citizens like all the saints and part of God's household. You are part of a building that has the apostles and prophets for its foundation and Christ Jesus himself for its main cornerstone" (Eph 2:19-20).

"What you have come to is Mount Zion and the city of the living God, the heavenly Jerusalem, where millions of angels have gathered for the festival, with the whole church in which everyone is a 'first-born son' and a citizen of heaven" (Heb 12:22-23).

PAULINE THEME THREE: CHRISTIAN UNITY

It is the Christian's union with Christ that underlies all his/her dignity and hope. The primary duty of each believer is to further the unity of head and members.

"The church is his body; he is its head" (Col 1:18).

"Be united in your convictions and united in your love, with a common purpose and a common mind ... There must be no competition among you, no conceit. Everybody is to be self-effacing. Always consider the other person to be better than yourself, so that nobody thinks of his own interests first but everybody thinks of other people's interest instead" (Phil 2:2-4).

"I appeal to you, brothers, for the sake of our Lord Jesus Christ, to make up the differences between you and instead of disagreeing among yourselves, to be united again in your belief and practice" (1 Cor 1:1).

"There is a variety of gifts, but always the same Spirit. There are all sorts of service to be done, but always to the same Lord, working in all sorts of different ways in different people. It is the same God who is working in all of them" (1 Cor 12:5-6).

"Just as a human body, though it is made up of many parts, is a single entity because all these parts, though many, make one body, so it is with Christ ... nor is the body to be identified with any one of its many parts ... God puts all the separate parts into the body on purpose ... what is more, it is precisely the parts of the body that seem to be

118

the weakest which are the indispensable ones ... now you together are Christ's body; but each of you is a different part of it. In the church, God has given the first place to apostles, the second to prophets, the third to teachers. After them, miracles and after them the gift of healing, helpers, good leaders, those with many languages" (1 Cor 12:12-30).

"There are no more distinctions between Jew and Greek, slave and free, male and female, but all of you are one in Christ Jesus" (Gal 3:28).

"I implore you to lead a life worthy of your vocation. Bear with one another charitably, in complete selflessness, gentleness and patience. Do all you can to preserve the unity of the Spirit by the peace that binds you together. There is one Body, one Spirit, just as you were all called into the one and the same hope when you were called. There is one Lord, one faith, one baptism and one God who is Father of all ..." (Eph 4:1-6).

"You should be clothed in sincere compassion, in kindness and humility, gentleness and patience. Bear with one another; forgive each other as soon as a quarrel begins ... over all these clothes ... put on love. And may the peace of Christ reign in your hearts, because it is for this that you were called together as parts of one body" (Col 3:12-15).

"Be at peace among yourselves ... warn idlers, give courage to those who are apprehensive, care for the weak and be patient with everyone. Make sure that people do not try to take revenge; you must all think of what is best for each other and for the community" (1 Thes 5:14-18).

"Obey your leaders and do as they tell you, because they must give an account of the way they look after your souls; make it a joy for them to do so and not a grief" (Heb 13:17).

"Stand firm and keep the traditions that we taught you, whether by mouth or by letter" (2 Thes 1:15).

"Keep away from any of the brothers who refuses to work or live according to the tradition we pass on to you" (2 Thes 3:6).

"If anyone refuses to obey ... have nothing to do with him, so that he will feel that he is in the wrong, though you are not to regard him as an enemy, but as a brother in need of correction" (2 Thes 3:13-15).

"You should not associate with a brother Christian who is leading an immoral life, or is a usurer, or idolatrous, or a slanderer, or a drunkard, or is dishonest; you should not even eat a meal with people like that" (1 Cor 5:11-12).

PAULINE THEME FOUR: CHRISTIAN LOVE AND VIRTUE

The union of Christians among themselves is a prelude to the effective evangelization of others, carried out by word and example. The example is more effective, although Christians should strive for the ability to explain why they act as they do.

"Make it a point of living quietly, attending to your own business, earning your own living" (1 Thes 4:11).

"Let your tolerance be evident to everyone ... fill your minds with everything that is true, noble, good and pure, everything we love and honor, everything that can be thought virtuous or worthy of praise" (Phil 3:17-21).

"Whatever you eat, whatever you drink, whatever you do at all, do it for the glory of God ... never do anything offensive to anyone ... try to be helpful to everyone at all times" (1 Cor 10:31-33).

"Love is always patient and kind; it is never jealous; it is never boastful or conceited; it is never rude or selfish; it does not take offense and is not resentful. Love takes no pleasure in other people's sins but delights in the truth. It is always ready to excuse, to trust, to hope and to endure whatever comes" (1 Cor 13:4-7).

"Christ Jesus comforts us in all our sorrows so that we can offer others, in their sorrows, the consolation that we have received from God ourselves" (2 Cor 1:4).

"Don't model yourselves on the behavior of the world around you, but let your behavior change, modeled by your new mind ... I urge each one among you not to exaggerate his real importance ... do not let your love be a pretense but sincerely prefer good to evil ... bless those who persecute you; never curse them, bless them. Rejoice with those who rejoice and be sad with those in sorrow. Treat everyone with equal kindness; never be condescending but make real friends with the poor. Do not allow yourself to become self-satisfied ... let everyone see that you are interested only in the highest ideals. Do all you can to live at peace with everyone" (Rom 12:3-23).

"Obey the governing authorities ... not only because you are afraid of being punished, but also for conscience's sake. This is also the reason why you must pay taxes" (Rom 13:1-7).

"Your mind must be renewed by a spiritual revolution so that you can put on the new self that has been created in God's way, in the goodness and holiness of the truth. So from now on there must be no more lies; you must speak the truth to one another ... never let the sun set on your anger ... stop stealing; find useful manual work instead ... let your words be for the improvement of others ... never have grudges, or lose your temper, or raise your voice ... be friends, be kind and forgiving ..." (Eph 5:17-32).

"This may be a wicked age, but your lives should redeem it. Do not be thoughtless but recognize what is the will of the Lord: among you there must be not even a mention of fornication or impurity in any of its forms, or promiscuity ... no coarseness or salacious talk and jokes ... don't drug yourselves with wine ..." (Eph 5:3-18).

"Continue to love each other like brothers ... welcome strangers; keep in mind those who are in prison ... honor marriage ... put greed out of your lives and be content with whatever you have ... behave honorably in everything you do" (Heb 13:1-19).

"You must consider yourselves to be dead to sin but alive for God in Christ Jesus. That is why you must not let sin reign in your mortal bodies or command your obedience to bodily passions" (Rom 6:11-12).

"Fasten your attention on holiness, faith, love and peace in union with all who call on the Lord with pure minds" (2 Tm 2:22).

"Don't lose sight of Jesus, who for sake of the joy in the future endured the cross" (Heb 12:2).

"What God wants is for you to be holy ... to use your body in an honorable way ..." (1 Thes 4:3-6).

"To be circumcised or uncircumcised means nothing. What does matter is to keep the commandments of God" (1 Cor 7:19).

"Keep on working at the Lord's work, knowing that in the Lord you can't be laboring in vain" (1 Cor 15:58).

"If you are guided by the Spirit, you will be in no danger of yielding to self-indulgence ... What the Spirit brings is: love, joy, peace, patience, kindness, goodness, trustfulness, gentleness and self-control. There can be no law against things like that, of course. You can't belong to Christ Jesus, unless you crucify all self-indulgent passions and desires" (Gal 5:16-26).

"The reason Christ died for all was so that the living should no longer live for themselves, but for him who died and was raised to life for them" (2 Cor 5:14-15).

PAULINE THEME FIVE: CHRISTIAN SALVATION

While the practice of virtue is expected of Christians and furthers the kingdom of God, it is not the primary cause of their salvation. Salvation is a free, unmerited gift of God, given to all people through the life, passion, death and resurrection of Jesus Christ.

Paul, particularly in his letters to the Galatians and Romans, points out that no human being can merit salvation. All people are slaves of sin. All need to be liberated by God's power and mercy. Paul's doctrine of salvation is in keeping with the whole of the Old Testament, where the people, because of their infidelity, would be doomed to perpetual slavery in Egypt, Assyria and Babylon, without the special intervention of Yahweh.

Paul also pointed out that the Law, which Yahweh gave to his people through Moses, indicated what was good, but it did not give any internal power to its devotees, so they might observe it. Yet Moses said that whoever did not keep the whole law was cursed. Christ took the curse upon himself, for the Scriptures also said that he who hung on a tree was cursed. The curse died with Christ on the cross. By rising from the dead, Christ established a new view of things. He, not the Law, brought life. Those who believed in him would have their sins forgiven and could enter eternal life.

Cooperation with the free gift of God, however, is still required. The practice of virtue, in imitation of Christ, is still an essential condition for salvation; but it is not the cause of it. Christ is the savior; we merely cooperate with him by following the path of holiness he has marked out for us.

"God has taken us out of the power of darkness and created a place

123

for us in the kingdom of the Son that he loves. In him we gain our freedom, the forgiveness of our sins" (Col 1:14).

"We acknowledge that what makes a man righteous is not obedience to the Law, but faith in Jesus Christ. We had to become believers in Christ Jesus no less than you had to. Now we hold that faith in Christ, rather than fidelity to the Law, is what justifies us, and that no one can be justified by keeping the Law" (Gal 2:15-16).

"Jews and Greeks are all under sin's dominion. As scripture says: 'There is not a good man left, no, not one; there is not one who understands, not one who looks to God.' Now all this that the Law says is said, as we know, for the benefit of those who are subject to the Law, but it is meant to silence everyone and to lay the whole world open to God's judgment. This is because no one can be justified in the sight of God by keeping the Law. All that law does is to tell us what is sinful" (Rom 3:9-20).

"Both Jew and pagan sinned and forfeited God's glory. Both are justified through the free gift of his grace by being redeemed in Christ Jesus, who was appointed by God to sacrifice his life so as to win reconciliation through faith" (Rom 3:23-24).

"It is through grace that you have been saved ... through faith; not by anything of your own, but by a gift from God" (Eph 2:6-9).

"You must live your whole life according to the Christ you have received" (Col 2:6).

"You have been buried with him, when you were baptized; and by baptism, too, you have been raised up with him through your belief in the power of God, who raised him from the dead" (Col 2:12).

"Through the blood of Jesus we have the right to enter the sanctuary, by a new way which he has opened for us, a living opening through the curtain, that is to say, his body ... Let us keep firm in the hope we

124

profess, because the one who made the promise is faithful. Let us be concerned for each other to stir a response in love and good works" (Heb 10:19-25).

"Only faith can guarantee the blessings that we hope for, or prove the existence of the realities that at present remain unseen. It was for faith that our ancestors were commended. It is impossible to please God without faith, since anyone who comes to him must believe that he exists and rewards those who try to find him" (Heb 11:1-6).

"Work for your salvation in fear and trembling" (Phil 2:13).

"All the runners at the stadium are trying to win, but only one of them gets the prize ... all the fighters at the games go into strict training ... that is how I run, intent on winning; that is how I fight, not beating the air. I treat my body hard and make it obey me, for, having been an announcer myself, I should not want to be disqualified" (1 Cor 9:24-27).

"Take as your models everybody who is already doing this (disciplining themselves to gain the prize of eternal life). There are many who are behaving as the enemies of the cross of Christ. They are destined to be lost" (Phil 3:17-18).

"The language of the cross may be illogical to those who are not on the way to salvation. But those of us who are on the way, see it as God's power to save" (1 Cor 1:18).

CHAPTER TEN

IMAGES OF GOD IN OTHER APOSTOLIC LETTERS

Seven letters of the Apostles have been accepted as divinely inspired writings since the second century. These letters, one by James, two by Peter, three by John and one by Jude are all included in the New Testament.

Although the apostolic letters were written over a span of forty years, they all exhort Christian believers to persevere in virtue, especially in charity to one another, even in the face of hostility from non-believers. They also encourage loyalty to the leaders of the Christian communities, rather than to self-appointed prophets. As Christians viewed Christ, the teacher, speaking through the letters of Paul, so they have listened to him speaking to them through these sacred letters. Jesus, the Teacher, is the dominating image of the letters.

Four great themes emerge from these letters, although there are some minor ones as well.

THEME ONE: ATTITUDE TOWARD PERSECUTION

When Christ walked with his apostles, he predicted his own persecution and that of his followers. "You will be hated by all men on account of my name; but the man who stands firm to the end will be saved" (Mt 10:17-25).

He told his followers to rejoice and not to despair when this happened. "Happy are you when people abuse you and persecute you and speak all kinds of calumny against you on my account. Rejoice and be glad, for your reward will be great in heaven; this is how they persecuted the prophets before you" (Mt 5:11-12).

When persecution came from both Jewish and Roman authorities, the apostles reminded their followers of a number of great truths:

- The persecution had been foreseen and was permitted by God for his own purposes.
- Christ was with his people in their trials.
- The trials tested and purified a believer's faith in Christ and in his promises.
- The faithful would overcome their persecutors by their perseverance in virtue under duress.
- Christ would reward them with the gift of eternal life.

"My brothers, you will always have your trials, but when they come, try to treat them as a happy privilege. You understand that your faith is only put to the test to make you patient. But patience too is to have its practical results so that you will become fully developed, complete, with nothing missing" (Jas 1:2-4).

"Happy the man who stands firm when trials come. He has proved himself, and will win the prize of life, the crown that the Lord has promised to those who love him" (Jas 1:12).

"If you have to suffer for being good, count it a blessing ... if it is the will of God that you should suffer, it is better to suffer for doing right than for doing wrong ... Think of what Christ suffered in this life and then arm yourselves with the same resolution that he had. Anyone who in this life has bodily suffering has broken with sin, because for the rest of his life on earth he is not ruled by human passions but only by the will of God" (1 Pt 3:14,17, 4:1-2).

"Be calm but vigilant, because your enemy the devil is prowling around like a roaring lion, looking for someone to eat. Stand up to him, strong in faith and in the knowledge that your brothers all over the world are suffering the same things. You will have to suffer only for a little while. The God of all grace who called you to eternal glory in Christ will see that all is well again. He will confirm, strengthen and support you. His power lasts for ever and ever" (2 Pt 5:8-11).

THEME TWO: THE PRACTICE OF VIRTUE:

Those who claim to be followers of Christ must lead holy lives: lives distinguished especially by charity. This is how all people, particularly our enemies, will come to recognize Christ living in us.

"My children, do not let anyone lead you astray: to live a holy life is to be holy just as God is holy ... In this way we distinguish the children of God from the children of the devil: anybody not living a holy life and not loving his brother is no child of God's" (1 Jn 3:7,10).

"My children, our love is not to be just words or mere talk, but something real and active. Only by this can we be certain that we are children of the truth" (1 Jn 3,18-19).

"My dear brothers: be quick to listen, but slow to speak and slow to rouse your temper ... Nobody must imagine that he is religious while he still goes on deceiving himself and not keeping control over his tongue; anyone who does this has the wrong idea of religion. Pure, unspoiled religion, in the eyes of God our Father is this: coming to the help of orphans and widows when they need it and keeping oneself uncontaminated by the world" (Jas 1:19,26-27).

"If one of the brothers or one of the sisters is in need of clothes and has not enough food to live on and one of you says to them: 'I wish you well; keep yourself warm and eat plenty,' without giving them these bare necessities of life, then what good is that? Faith is like that. If good works do not go with it, it is quite dead" (Jas 2:15-17).

"Be patient, brothers, until the Lord's coming. Think of a farmer. How patiently he waits for the precious fruit of the ground until it has had the spring and the autumn rains! You too have to be patient; do not lose heart, because the Lord's coming will be soon ... For your example, brothers, in submitting with patience, take the prophets who spoke in the name of the Lord. Remember it is those who had endurance that we say are the blessed ones. You have heard of the patience of Job and understood the Lord's purpose, realizing that the Lord is kind and compassionate" (Jas 5:7-11).

"Do not behave in the way that you liked to before you learned the truth. Make a habit of obedience; be holy in all you do, since it is the Holy One who has called you and scripture says: 'Be holy, for I am holy.' " (1 Pt 1:14-16).

"I urge you, my dear people, while you are visitors and pilgrims, to keep yourselves free from selfish passions that attack the soul. Always behave honorably among pagans so that they can see your good works for themselves and when the day of reckoning comes, give thanks to God for the things which now make them denounce you as criminals" (1 Pt 2:11-12).

"God has given us the guarantee of something very great and wonderful to come ... but to attain this, you will have to do your utmost yourselves, adding goodness to the faith that you have, understanding to your goodness, self-control to your understanding, patience to your self-control, true devotion to your patience, kindness toward your fellow men to your devotion and, to this kindness, love" (2 Pt 1:4-7).

"We can be sure that we know God only by keeping his commandments. Anyone who says, 'I know him,' and does not keep his commandments is a liar, refusing to admit the truth" (1 Jn 2:3-4).

"If a man who was rich enough in this world's goods saw that one of his brothers was in need, but closed his heart to him, how could the love of God be living in him?" (1 Jn 3:17).

"We can be sure that we love God's children if we love God himself and do what he has commanded us. This is what loving God is:

129

keeping his commandments" (1 Jn 5:2-3).

"For the sake of the Lord, accept the authority of every social institution ... God wants you to be good citizens, so as to silence what fools are saying in their ignorance" (1 Pt 2:13-16).

"In the same way, wives should be obedient to their husbands ... husbands must always treat their wives with consideration ..." (1 Pt 3:1,7).

"Agree among yourselves and be sympathetic. Love the brothers. Have compassion and be self-effacing. Never pay back one wrong with another, or an angry word with another one. Instead, pay back with a blessing. That is what you are called to do, so that you inherit a blessing yourself" (1 Pt 3:8-9).

THEME THREE: PRESERVING UNITY

A true follower of Christ is concerned not only with his personal union with Christ, but with other members of Christ's body as well. The unity of Christians in faith and charity provides a powerful common witness to Christ and sustains the fervor of believers. Unity, therefore, is something to be prayed for and striven for, while disunity in belief or practice is an evil to be avoided at all costs.

"My brothers, do not try to combine faith in Jesus Christ, our glorified Lord, with the making of distinctions between classes of people ... as soon as you make distinctions between classes of people, you are committing sin and under condemnation for breaking the Law" (Jas 2:1,9).

"Wherever you find jealousy and ambition, you will find disharmony and wicked things of every kind being done; whereas the wisdom that comes down from above is essentially something pure; it also makes for peace and is kindly and considerate. It is full of compassion and

130

shows itself by doing good. Nor is there any trace of partiality or hypocrisy in it" (Jas 3:16-17).

"Where do these wars and battles between yourselves first start? Isn't it precisely in the desires fighting inside your own selves? You want something and you haven't got it; so you are prepared to kill. You have an ambition that you cannot satisfy; so you fight to get your way by force ... Humble yourselves before the Lord and he will lift you up" (Jas 4:1-2,10).

"Brothers, do not slander one another. Anyone who slanders a brother, or condemns him, is speaking against the Law and condemning the Law" (Jas 4:11).

"If any one of you is in trouble, he should pray. If anyone is feeling happy, he should sing a psalm. If one of you is ill, he should send for the elders of the church and they must anoint him with oil in the name of the Lord and pray over him" (Jas 5:13-14).

"Be sure you are never spiteful, or deceitful, or hypocritical, or envious and critical of each other. You are newborn and like babies, you should be hungry for nothing but milk--the spiritual honesty which will help you to grow up to salvation" (1 Pt 2:1-3).

"I have something to tell you elders: Be shepherds of the flock of God that is entrusted to you. Watch over it, not simply as a duty but gladly, because God wants it. Not for sordid money, but because you are eager to do it. Never be a dictator over any group that is put in your charge, but be an example that the whole flock can follow" (1 Pt 5:1-4).

"To the rest of you I say: do what the elders tell you and wrap yourselves in humility to be servants of each other ... be calm but vigilant" (1 Pt 5:5,8).

"As there were false prophets in the past history of our people, so you

131

too will have your false teachers, who will insinuate their own disruptive views ... especially those who are governed by their corrupt bodily desires and have no respect for authority ... self-willed people with no reverence ... people who insult ... men who amuse themselves by deceiving you ... those who promise freedom but are themselves slaves" (2 Pt 2).

"If we acknowledge our sins, then God who is faithful and just will forgive our sins and purify us from everything that is wrong" (1 Jn 1:9).

"Children, these are the last days. You were told that an Antichrist must come and now several antichrists have already appeared ... the man who denies that Jesus is the Christ--he is the liar; he is the Antichrist ... Keep alive in yourselves what you were taught in the beginning ... Live in Christ, then, my children, so that if he appears, we may have full confidence and not turn from him in shame at his coming" (1 Jn 2:18-28).

"If anybody does not keep within the teaching of Christ but goes beyond it, he cannot have God with him. Only those who keep to what he taught can have the Father and the Son with them. If anyone comes to you bringing a different doctrine, you must not receive him in your house or even give him a greeting" (2 Jn 1:9-10).

"These people (the false teachers) not only defile their bodies and disregard authority ... they abuse anything they do not understand ... They are shamelessly only looking after themselves. They are mischief-makers, grumblers governed only by their own desire, with mouths full of boastful talk, ready with flattery for other people when they see some advantage in it" (Jude 1:8-16).

THEME FOUR: CHRISTIAN DIGNITY

As long as Christians remember the nobility of their call, and pray to live up to it, they will find the interior strength and courage they need to be faithful to Christ.

"You are a chosen race, a royal priesthood, a consecrated nation, a people set apart to sing the praises of God who called you out of the darkness into his wonderful light. Once you were not a people at all. Now you are the People of God. Once you were outside the mercy. Now you have been given mercy" (2 Pt 2:9-10).

"Think of the love that the Father has lavished on us, by letting us be called God's children; and that is what we are. Because the world refused to acknowledge him, therefore it does not acknowledge us. My dear people, we are already the children of God, but what we are to be in the future has not yet been revealed. All we know is, that when it is revealed we shall be like him, because we shall see him as he really is" (1 Jn 3:1-2).

CHAPTER ELEVEN

IMAGES OF GOD IN THE BOOK OF REVELATION

Scholars believe that the writer of the Book of Revelations was probably a disciple of John, the evangelist, who wrote in the latter part of the first century. The work is a meditation on the prophecies of Jesus concerning the destruction of Jerusalem and the end of the world. The symbolism used is similar to that found in Ezekiel and Daniel.

The destruction of Jerusalem had already taken place, verifying the words of Christ. All that remained to be validated were cataclysmic events heralding the second coming of Christ. The author of Revelation believed these were imminent, since the persecution of Christians, with all its suffering, seemed to him a prelude to the end of the world.

The author personally experienced these sufferings. To encourage others, he shared with them a series of visions in which he saw the triumphant Redeemer and heard his promises of victory to those who endured. In these visions evil rulers and their empires are swept away: new heavens and earth are formed. The faithful (saints) who had persevered now join in the triumph of Christ (the Lamb). They live with him in the New Jerusalem, the heavenly city, where all is beautiful, perfect, peaceful and full of joy.

While some of the symbolism in the book is difficult to explain, the general message is clear: Christ has triumphed over his enemies. Those who remain faithful to him will one day share in his victory and joy. As the author himself expresses it: "He loves us and has washed away our sins with his blood and made us a line of kings, priests to serve his God and Father ... It is he who is coming on the clouds; everyone will see him, even those who pierced him and all the races of the earth will mourn over him. This is the truth. Amen. 'I am the Alpha and the Omega,' says the Lord God, who is, who was

134

and who is to come, the Almighty" (Rv 1:5-8).

The Book of Revelation contains two striking images which have fascinated the imaginations of writers and artists over the centuries.

Christ Victorious King of Kings

Although the first three chapters address seven churches in Asia Minor, the messages speak of Christ's victory over sin and death. They encourage all Christians to persevere in their faith, so that they may one day share in the joys of Christ's victory.

Each message comes from Christ, now arrayed in splendor:
"I heard a voice behind me, shouting like a trumpet ... I turned around to see who had spoken to me ... and I saw a figure like a Son of man dressed in a long robe tied at the waist with a golden girdle. His head and his hair were white as white wool or as snow, his eyes like a burning flame, his feet like burnished bronze ... and his voice like the sound of the ocean.... 'It is I, the First and the Last; I am the Living One. I was dead and now I am to live for ever and ever. I hold the keys of death and of the underworld. Now write down all that you see of present happenings and things that are still to come...' " (Rv 1:9-20).

-Ephesus: "I know all about you: how hard you work and how much you put up with ... that you have patience and have suffered for my name without growing tired. Nevertheless, I have this complaint to make: You have less love now than you used to. Think where you were before you fell. Repent and do as you used to at first" (Rv 2:2-5).

-Smyrna: "Even if you have to die, keep faithful and I will give you the crown of life for your prize" (Rv 2:11).

-Pergamum: "To those who prove victorious, I will give the hidden manna and a white stone--a stone with a new name written on it" (a

135

trophy given to Olympic winners) (Rv 2:17).

-Thyatira: "To those who prove victorious, I will give the morning star" (a symbol of the resurrection) (Rv 2:28).

-Sardis: "Those who prove victorious will be dressed in white robes" (a symbol of pure joy) (Rv 3:5).

-Philadelphia: "Those who prove victorious, I will make into pillars in the sanctuary of my God" (a symbol of permanency in God's presence) (Rv 3:12).

-Laodicea: "Those who prove victorious, I will allow to share my throne" (a symbol of sharing power over everything in the new kingdom) (Rv 3:21)

Christ the Victorious Lamb

In the next section of the book--chapters four through eleven--John speaks of things that will precede the great day of victory for God's people. Christ, symbolized by a slain lamb that now lives, opens the book of life to reveal to believers that all things have meaning, including suffering, if they remain faithful to God and persevere in love, for there will be a resurrection of the just and unjust. This great truth, confirmed by the resurrection of Jesus, was hidden from the foundation of the world (Rv 4-5).

"I saw a powerful angel who called with a loud voice: 'Is there anyone worthy to open the scroll and break the seals of it?' But there was no one, in heaven or on the earth or under the earth who was able to open the scroll and read it. I wept bitterly because there was nobody fit to open the scroll and read it, but one of the elders said to me: 'There is no need to cry: the Lion of the tribe of Judah, the Root of David, has triumphed and he will open the scroll and the seven seals of it. The Lamb came forward to take the scroll from the right hand of the One sitting on the throne" (Rv 5:2-7).

Believers, alongside unbelievers, will suffer in wars, from famine, plague and persecutors (symbolized by the four horsemen). They may think these evils will never end, but they will. When the full number of the elect is gathered, the end spoken of by Jesus will come (Rv 6).

The full number of the elect will include the remnant of Israel, spoken of by the prophets. In chapter seven John speaks of 12,000 from each tribe ... 144,000 from all twelve. Rather than a mere mathematical calculation, this represents a symbol of completeness.

Joined to these will be a throng, impossible to count: "After that I saw a huge number, impossible to count, of people from every nation, race, tribe and language; they were standing in front of the throne and in front of the Lamb, dressed in white robes and holding palms in their hands. They shouted aloud, 'Victory to our God, who sits on the throne and to the Lamb!' " (Rv 7).

All these faithful ones will rejoice forever and ever with the Lord. "They will never hunger or thirst again; neither the sun nor scorching wind will ever plague them, because the Lamb who is at the throne will be their shepherd and will lead them to springs of living water; and God will wipe away all tears from their eyes" (Rv 7:16-17).

The prayers of the faithful help shorten the time of waiting. "Another angel, who had a golden censer, came and stood at the altar. A large quantity of incense was given to him to offer with the prayers of all the saints on the golden altar that stood in front of the throne; and so from the angel's hand the smoke of the incense went up in the presence of God and with it the prayers of the saints" (Rv 8:3-4).

Chapters eight through ten describe in symbolic language the terrible things that those dominated by sin will do to people and to the things of nature as well. However, the fullness of time will eventually arrive and Christ will return to judge the living and the dead. "Then the angel that I had seen, standing on the sea and the land, raised his right hand to heaven and swore by the One who lives forever and ever and made heaven and all that is in it and the earth and all it bears, and the sea and all it holds, 'The time of waiting is over. At the time when the seventh angel is heard sounding his trumpet, God's secret intentions will be fulfilled, just as he announced in the Good News told to his servants, the prophets.' " (Rv 10:5-7).

"Then the seventh angel blew his trumpet and voices could be heard shouting in heaven, calling: 'The kingdom of the world has become the kingdom of our Lord and his Christ and he will reign forever and ever.' The twenty-four elders, enthroned in the presence of God, prostrated themselves and touched the ground with their foreheads worshiping God with these words: "We give thanks to you, Almighty Lord God, He-Is-and-He-Was, for using your great power and beginning your reign. The nations were seething with rage and now the time has come for your own anger, and for the dead to be judged and for your servants the prophets, for the saints and for all who worship you, small or great, to be rewarded. The time has come to destroy those who are destroying the earth.' " (Rv 11:15-18).

The followers of Christ are enmeshed in an ancient struggle between good and evil, which began before human beings were created. The struggle between good and evil spirits ended with the defeat of the devil and his followers, who have now set out to entice human beings to turn away from God. "Let the heavens rejoice and all who live there; but for you, earth and sea, trouble is coming, because the devil has gone down to you in a rage, knowing that his days are numbered" (Rv 12:12).

The followers of goodness rally around a child sent from heaven (Christ). Those who refuse to worship the beasts (tyrants who aid the devil) will prevail, while the rulers and their glorious kingdoms will vanish (Rv 13-14).

Those who persevere will rejoice with all those who have remained faithful to Christ: "Alleluia! The reign of the Lord our God Almighty has begun. Let us be glad and joyful and give praise to God, because this is the time for the marriage of the Lamb. His bride is ready and she has been able to dress herself in dazzling white linen, because her linen is made of the good deeds of the saints" (Rv 19:7-8).

The faithful will live with the Victorious Lamb in a new heaven and on a new earth. "You see this city? Here God lives among men. He will make his home among them; they shall be his people and he will be their God. His name is God-with-them. He will wipe away all tears from their eyes. There will be no more death and no more mourning or sadness. The world of the past has gone" (Rv 21:3-4).

Christ the Beautiful Temple of God

The book ends with a description of the magnificent city of God, where all the faithful will live in perfect happiness with their Creator and Redeemer. The symbolism comes directly from chapter forty of Ezekiel. "Happy are those who will have washed their robes clean, so that they will have the right to feed on the tree of life and can come through the gates into the city" (Rev 22:14).

The ending of Revelation brings us back the yearning expressed by the Psalmist: "One thing I ask of Yahweh, one thing I seek: to live in the house of Yahweh all the days of my life, to enjoy the sweetness of Yahweh and to consult him in his Temple ... I will offer exultant sacrifice. I will sing. I will play for Yahweh!" (Ps 27:4-6).

CHAPTER TWELVE

UNDERSTANDING THE REVEALED IMAGES OF GOD

The Hebrews, to whom God chose to reveal himself, began their lives as desert nomads and wound up as settled town dwellers. Their images of God naturally reflect this transition. They also depict him in the basic relationships of society: father, friend, lover, bridegroom, husband, servant. As a desert people the Hebrews were closely in touch with nature. This is readily seen in their mental pictures of God as Creator, Provider, Wonderworker, Kinsman, Chieftain, Victorious Leader, Generous Host, and Shepherd. We see it also in their descriptions of Yahweh as an eagle or hen guiding and protecting its young, as a lamb that gives up its wool and flesh uncomplainingly that the people might live.

The desert Hebrews saw Yahweh as a cloud, tent, breeze that offered shelter and relief, as a shield and high rock that offered protection. As they became more settled, the sacred Hebrew writers referred to Yahweh as King, Ruler, Teacher, Overseer, Peacemaker, Judge, Healer, Gardener, Vinegrower, Potter, Stonemason, Bleacher, Silversmith. The city-dweller appreciated God as his fortress, walled city, temple, road, vine, bread, water, light.

While one may argue over the arrangement of some of the above categories, it's clear that God appeals to people in images drawn from the circumstances of their lives. And while all of the revealed images have the potential of stimulating our feelings about God, not all affect everyone in the same way, or to the same degree. Rural people may find the desert images more appealing. City dwellers may find the urban images more compelling. Tradesmen may relate to another image. The important truth to keep in mind as you reflect on these texts is:

GOD CONTINUES TO REVEAL HIMSELF
TO ALL HUMAN BEINGS
THROUGH IMAGES WHICH APPEAL TO THEM

Public revelation may be over, but private revelations never cease. God continues to speak to each person not only through the Scriptures, but also through the myriad of his creatures, through our fellow human beings, through personal experiences (both pleasant and unpleasant), through his official ministers, through good books, through scientific data, through everything!

The principal obstacle confronting us in our quest to know God is not his silence, but our inability to listen ... our unwillingness to reflect ... our impatience and busyness.

It seems that God has revealed himself to certain people in certain ways, not to restrict us in our ways of "seeing" him, but to sensitize our imaginations and stimulate our sense of discovery. God is all around us and in us as well. As Paul said: "He is not far from any of us, since it is in him that we live and move and exist" (Acts 17:28).

To the extent that we really believe this, we will make time for God, time to reflect on his word, on his creation, on his people, on his plans for our happiness ... time to enter into God!

All the saints had their favorite images of God, but this does not mean that they ignored or belittled other images. However, their chosen image was one that quickly and easily brought them into the presence of God, enabling them to remain in his presence for extended periods of time.

Like the saints, each of us has particular images of God that we find attractive and helpful, and God wants us to utilize them. If we do, we will find that he speaks to our hearts through them.

CHAPTER THIRTEEN

IMAGES OF GOD IN CHURCH HISTORY

In the early art of the church the image of Christ as the Good Shepherd seems to have held great appeal.

The Eastern churches of Christianity found that the image of Christ, Lord and King of Everything, swayed their minds and hearts. The icons which artists created bespeak a gentle majesty that has not lost its appeal through the centuries. Indeed, as the Western Christian churches came under the domination of kings and princes, the image of Christ, the King, the Lord of Lords, appealed to them as well.

When terrible plagues and wars swept through Europe, the image of the Crucified Savior emerged as a favorite for people. It brought them consolation and hope in their sufferings.

Since the Sixteen Century the great mystical writers have all been attracted by the suffering Christ. They have had particular devotion to his five wounds, the blood he shed, his wounded heart. St. Margaret Mary helped popularize Christ under the image of the Sacred Heart.

All the Popes of modern times have praised the image of Christ as the Sacred Heart. They show that the roots of this image and devotion are scriptural. They encourage believers to make use of this image in prayer, because it can bring them quickly and easily to the very core of understanding God, for God is love; and all he does is done in love.

Since Vatican II the image of Christ, the Risen Lord, has emerged more and more in churches and in pictorial art. This is in keeping with the whole thrust of that great council: renewal, transformation, hope. The Risen Christ stands in the midst of the faithful, reaffirming their belief in life after death. He proclaims the victory of those who remain faithful to him. He silences those who claim he was just another wise human teacher who passed away. He offers hope to the masses of unimportant, forgotten men and women. He rebukes those who place all their trust in the things of this present life.

What image will appeal most to the people of the 21st century? Who knows? It will undoubtedly evolve from the scriptures and arise from the needs of the majority of people. Nevertheless, many people will continue to feel lost, unloved, controlled by others; so the images of the Good Shepherd, the Sacred Heart, the Gentle King, the Risen Lord will undoubtedly continue to touch their hearts and dispose them to listen to what Christ reveals for their peace.

The Catholic Church uses and will continue to use all these images in her liturgical prayers to assist her sons and daughters to pray. Those who take the time to examine her public prayers will discover a veritable treasure trove of inspired and inspiring thoughts that have the potential of arousing and sustaining their private prayer life as well.

In the following section I offer a sampling of these spiritual masterpieces, selected from the liturgical year and the official prayerbook of the Catholic Church, the breviary. Through these she celebrates the mystery of salvation which began with the promise of God to help us, and which continues in our own day and will continue until the last day.

CHAPTER FOURTEEN

IMAGES OF GOD IN LITURGICAL PRAYER

Over the centuries the Catholic church has developed a great treasury of prayers which, in conjunction with the Scriptures, are used in public worship. These can stimulate our private prayer life as well, particularly when we feel unimaginative or weary.

Each prayer is a gem, created after much reflection and careful choice of phraseology. Each is a spiritual tune that lifts our spirits above the mundane. Each reminds us of some great truth. Each deepens our faith, hope and love. Many also make use of a particular image of God.

The few prayers offered here reveal a glimpse of their beauty. Hopefully, they will stimulate the reader to delve more fully into them and to use them as a source of personal prayer.

Advent: Jesus The Liberator

The church's yearly celebration of Christ, present in our time, commences in Advent. During this season we are called to reflect on the master-plan of God for our happiness, a plan that began long ago but that continues in time, a plan that calls for our personal liberation from sin and our rededication to God, a plan that will reach completion when Christ returns to earth in glory and power.

With our primeval parents and all their descendants, we long for freedom from evil and death. Jesus is our liberator, promised by the Father and spoken of by all the prophets. He is the Holy One who has triumphed over sin and death. He is the king who will rule over everything.

Those who listen to Christ and follow his example will likewise overcome sin and death. They will find great happiness and peace in

144

this life and the next. They will become a source of life for others, for Christ himself will be working in them and through them. He will one day raise them from the dead and share his rule over everything with them. The church's great Advent prayers bring all these inspiring thoughts to our minds.

"God of power and mercy, open our hearts in welcome. Remove the things that hinder us from receiving Christ with joy, so that we may share his wisdom and become one with him when he comes in glory" (2nd Sunday, Opening Prayer of the Missal).

"Lord, fill our hearts with your love. As you revealed to us by an angel the coming of your Son as man, so lead us through his suffering and death to the glory of his resurrection" (4th Sunday, Opening Prayer of the Missal).

Christmas: Jesus The Savior Among Us

During the Christmas season we recall the historical birth of our Savior, but also his renewed birth in the hearts of all who believe in him. His birth brought, and continues to bring, joy and hope to a world that is saddened by sin and downcast by despair. Those who believe in Christ and live as he taught experience his joy and freedom. They are likewise moved by God's Spirit to help others share their blessings.

The Christmas liturgies celebrate this joy and hope, as well as the impulse to share the Good News of Christ with others. Like the shepherds of old we are drawn by the kindness of God, we feel our hearts on fire with his love and consequently, we want others to know the good things that God has done for us and wishes to do for them as well.

"God of endless ages, Father of all goodness, we keep vigil for the dawn of salvation and the birth of your Son. With gratitude we recall his humanity, the life he shared with us. May the power of his

145

divinity help us answer his call to forgiveness and life" (Opening Prayer, Vigil Mass).

"Lord God, we praise you for creating us and still more for restoring us in Christ. Your Son shared our weakness. May we share his glory" (Opening Prayer, Christmas Day).

"Father, the child born today is the Savior of the world. He made us your children. May he welcome us into your kingdom" (Communion Prayer, Christmas Day).

"Father in heaven, creator of all, you ordered the earth to bring forth life and crowned its goodness by creating the human family. In history's moment, when all was ready, you sent your Son to dwell in time, obedient to the laws of life in our world. Teach us the sanctity of human love, show us the value of family life, and help us to live in peace with all people that we may share in your life forever" (Opening Prayer, Holy Family).

"Eternal Father, we want to live as Jesus, Mary and Joseph, in peace with you and one another. May this communion strengthen us to face the troubles of life" (Communion Prayer, Holy Family).

"God our Father, we celebrate at this season, the beginning of our salvation. On this feast of Mary, the Mother of God, we ask that our salvation will be brought to its fulfillment" (Prayer Over the Gifts, Jan. 1st).

"Father, you revealed your Son to the nations by the guidance of a star. Lead us to your glory in heaven by the light of faith" (Opening Prayer, Epiphany).

The Baptism And Public Life: Jesus Model Of Virtue

The Gospels indicate that the public life of Christ began when John baptized him in the Jordan River. In recalling that momentous event, we also recall our own baptism, in which the same Holy Spirit came upon us, to help us live with Christ and proclaim the Good News of God's love to others.

Effective evangelization always begins with example. So during this period of time we focus our attention on Christ, the master teacher and exemplar of all virtues. His tolerance, patience, mercy, gentleness, kindness are unmatched by any other human being in history. His parables reinforce his verbal teachings; his works of mercy and power cause even the most jaded to reflect. With the universal church, we pray that we might become more and more like him in our daily lives, so that his kingdom may come.

"Father in heaven, you revealed Christ as your Son by the voice that spoke over the waters of the Jordan. May all who share in the sonship of Christ follow in his path of service to others and reflect the glory of his kingdom, even to the ends of the earth" (Opening Prayer, Baptism of the Lord).

"Lord, you feed us with bread from heaven. May we hear your Son with faith and become your children in name and in fact" (Communion Prayer, Baptism of the Lord).

"Almighty and ever-present Father, your watchful care reaches from end to end and orders all things in such power that even the tensions and the tragedies of sin cannot frustrate your loving plans. Help us to embrace your will. Give us the strength to follow your call, so that your truth may live in our hearts and reflect peace to those who believe in your love" (Opening Prayer, 2nd Sunday, Ordinary Time).

"Lord our God, help us to love you with all our hearts and to love all people as you love them" (Opening Prayer, 4th Sunday).

"Father in heaven, the loving plan of your wisdom took flesh in Jesus Christ and changed mankind's history by his command of perfect love. May our fulfillment of his command reflect your wisdom and bring your salvation to the ends of the earth" (Opening Prayer, 6th Sunday).

"Father, keep before us the wisdom and love revealed in your Son. Help us to be like him in word and deed" (Opening Prayer, 7th Sunday).

"Lord, as you give us the body and blood of your Son, guide us with your Spirit that we may honor you not only with our lips, but also with the lives we lead, and so enter your kingdom" (Communion Prayer, 9th Sunday).

Lent: Jesus Conqueror Of Sin And Satan

The church, like a good mother, knows that although we are attracted by Christ, we are also attracted by the passing things of earth. She knows that we sometimes even prefer these to Christ. Our ancient enemy, the devil, has used the lures of pleasure, power and prestige to entice minds and hearts away from Christ. The Gospels relate that he even used these to tempt Christ to disobey his Father!

During the forty days of Lent, we recall the failure of the Chosen People to resist the lures of Satan and the consequences of their failure. We recall the triumph of Christ over the same temptations. We focus on the means that Christ and his believers have used successfully: fasting, prayer and works of charity.

Each of these spiritual tools is uniquely designed by God to counteract the allurements posed by the passing things of this world. Each deepens union with Christ and feeling for others.

Abstaining or fasting from food, drink and other bodily pleasures holds in check our desires for physical delights. It liberates the mind and heart. Sages through the centuries have known this, but Christ enables his followers to do this for a nobler reason: to maintain their

148

union with him and their zeal for his kingdom.

Prayer constantly reminds a person of his/her dependency on, and accountability to, God. It checks the desire for unlimited and unrestrained use of power. It keeps a person humble and service-orientated. It prevents a person from becoming insensitive and manipulative.

Almsgiving and other works of charity also serve to remind a person that all things are on loan, that true greatness is measured by generosity and service of others, not by the number of possessions and servants.

"Lord help us to resist temptation by our Lenten works of charity and penance. By this sacrifice may we be prepared to celebrate the death and resurrection of Christ our Savior and be cleansed from sin and renewed in spirit" (Prayer over the Gifts, Ash Wednesday).

"God our Father, teach us to find new life through penance. Keep us from sin and help us live by your commandment of love" (Opening prayer, Monday, 2nd Week).

"Father, you have taught us to overcome our sins by prayer, fasting and works of mercy. When we are discouraged by our weakness, give us confidence in your love" (Opening prayer, 3rd Sunday).

"Father, help us to be like Christ your son, who loved the world and died for our salvation. Inspire us by his love and guide us by his example" (Opening prayer, 5th Sunday).

Passiontide: Jesus Suffering Servant

The most solemn week of the church year begins on Palm Sunday and ends on Holy Saturday Evening. During that brief period we remember the awesome price Christ paid to reconcile us to the Father and to one another.

149

Christ had previously said that no greater love can be had than to give one's life for another. He lived his own words by laying down his life for us. He had also said that if he be lifted up, he would draw all things to himself. The image of the crucified Christ continues to impress the mind and change the hearts of people. People today, as well those of the past, can truly say with St. Paul: "He loved me and gave himself up for me" (Gal 2:21).

The Gospels make it clear that Christ was in charge of his fate throughout his terrible ordeal. No one took his life. He laid it down freely for our sake and resumed it again, also for our sake. Christ is the master of life, because he is the source of life. He does not wish the death of a sinner, but that he/she be converted and live.

Sin loses its power over us, when we know that we are forgiven, when we know that our present life is only the initial stage of eternal life. Christ brings such knowledge. He defeats the power of sin and death by bringing pardon, new life and hope. Passiontide is therefore a celebration of victory and hope, not a remembrance of defeat and despair.

"Lord, the death of your Son gives us hope and strengthens our faith. May his resurrection give us perseverance and lead us to salvation" (Communion Prayer, Palm Sunday).

"Lord, make us worthy to celebrate these mysteries. Each time we offer this memorial sacrifice the work of our redemption is accomplished" (Prayer Over the Gifts, Holy Thursday).

"Almighty and eternal God, you have restored us to life by the triumphant death and resurrection of Christ. Continue this healing work within us. May we who participate in this mystery never cease to serve you" (Prayer After Communion, Good Friday).

"Lord God, the creation of man was a wonderful work, his redemption still more wonderful. May we persevere in right reason against all that entices to sin and so attain to everlasting joy" (Prayer After Reading 1, Easter Vigil).

Easter: Jesus Risen Savior

As nature recovers from its long winter sleep and breaks into new bloom, the church celebrates on Easter Christ's triumph over the long reign of sin and death. Alleluia, Alleluia, Alleluia! Rejoice and be glad! He is risen from the sleep of death! Christ, the first-born of the dead, has triumphed over the ancient enemy of all human beings! Words like these ring out from communities of believers throughout the earth.

Christ now lives to intercede for us with the Father, that we may also triumph over sin and death. He pleads on our behalf through all who are united with him in Baptism. Hence, the transmission of Christ's life, through the sacrament of Baptism, occupies a position of central importance in the liturgy and prayers of Easter.

"God our Father, by raising Christ your Son you conquered the power of death and opened for us the way to eternal life. Let our celebration today raise us up and renew our lives by the Spirit that is within us" (Opening Prayer, Easter Sunday).

"Heavenly Father and God of mercy, we no longer look for Jesus among the dead, for he is alive and has become the Lord of life. From the waters of death you raise us with him and renew your gift of life within us. Increase in our minds and hearts the risen life we share with Christ and help us to grow as your people toward the fullness of eternal life with you" (Opening Prayer, 2nd Sunday of Easter).

"Lord, through faith and baptism we have become a new creation. Accept the offering of your people, and of those recently born again in baptism, and bring us to eternal happiness" (Prayer Over the Gifts, 2nd Sunday of Easter).

151

"God our Father, may we look forward with hope to our resurrection, for you have made us your sons and daughters, and restored the joy of our youth" (Opening Prayer, 3rd Sunday of Easter).

"Almighty and ever-living God, give us new strength from the courage of Christ our shepherd, and lead us to join the saints in heaven" (Opening Prayer, 4th Sunday of Easter).

"God our Father, look upon us with love. You redeem us and make us your children in Christ. Give us true freedom and bring us to the inheritance you promised" (Opening Prayer, 5th Sunday of Easter).

"Ever-living God, help us to celebrate our joy in the resurrection of the Lord and to express in our lives the love we celebrate" (Opening Prayer, 6th Sunday of Easter).

Ascension: Jesus The New Creation

The Acts of the Apostles tell us that, after his resurrection, Jesus appeared to his believers for a period of forty days. When that brief period ended, he met them on the Mount of Olives, outside Jerusalem, and from that hill ascended into the heavens out of sight (Acts 1). Jesus has returned to the Father, to prepare a place for those who believe in him, for those who love and serve him in others.

His followers were now required to walk by faith, and not by sight. Yet he would be with them, enlightening their minds and touching their hearts, as they make their personal journeys to the Father and the place he has prepared for them.

The liturgy and prayers of Ascension focus our minds on the glory that is to come for all who persevere in faith and love, glory that eye has not seen, ear has not heard, nor can the human mind even conceive.

"God our Father, make us joyful in the ascension of your Son, Jesus

Christ. May we follow him into the new creation, for his ascension is our glory and our hope" (Opening Prayer).

"Lord, receive our offering as we celebrate the ascension of Christ your Son. May his gifts help us rise with him to the joys of heaven" (Prayer Over the Gifts).

"Father, in this Eucharist, we touch the divine life you give to the world. Help us to follow Christ with love to eternal life where he is Lord forever and ever" (Communion Prayer).

Pentecost: Jesus The Spirit Of God

On the Feast of Pentecost the church celebrates the arrival of the Holy Spirit, which Jesus promised to send to help us understand his teachings and put them into practice (cf. Jn 16).

The Chosen People called the Feast of First Fruits Pentecost, because these were usually gathered in about fifty days after planting. With the arrival of the Holy Spirit upon the disciples of Jesus, fifty days after his resurrection, the feast took on new meaning.

The Holy Spirit is the first fruit received by believers from the ascended Christ. The community of believers, in turn, became the first fruits offered by Christ to the Father.

The Acts of the Apostles is sometimes called the Gospel of the Holy Spirit, because it describes the dramatic changes which the Holy Spirit effected in believers and in those to whom they preached the Good News. The changes and fruits continue, because the Holy Spirit remains as a permanent gift of Christ to his church. The Holy Spirit continues to fill the minds and hearts of the faithful with love and zeal for Christ and his kingdom.

As the symbols of light and water figured prominently in the liturgy and prayers of Easter, so the symbols of fire, wind and oil

153

predominate in the Feast of Pentecost. These symbols indicate radical change, outward movement, and strength which the Holy Spirit brings to believers in Christ.

The Ordinary Time after Pentecost (approximately half of the calendar year) focuses our attention on the life and teachings of Christ, with the confidence that the Holy Spirit will help us better understand and more faithfully live what we have come to believe is true, noble and good. It contains a variety of divine images.

"God our Father, let the Spirit you sent on your church to begin the teaching of the gospel continue to work in the world through the hearts of all who believe" (Opening Prayer, Pentecost).

"Father, you sent your Word to bring us truth and your Spirit to make us holy. Through them we come to know the mystery of your life. Help us to worship you, one God in three Persons, by proclaiming and living our faith in you" (Opening Prayer, Trinity Sunday).

"Almighty God, our hope and our strength, without you we falter. Help us to follow Christ and live according to your will" (Opening Prayer, 10th Sunday).

"Lord, be merciful to your people. Fill us with your gifts and make us always eager to serve you in faith, hope and love" (Opening Prayer, 15th Sunday).

"God our Father and Protector, without you nothing is holy, nothing has value. Guide us to everlasting life by helping us to use wisely the blessings you have given to the world" (Opening Prayer, 17th Sunday).

"Lord, may the Eucharist you give us bring us to salvation and keep us faithful to the light of your truth" (Communion Prayer, 19th Sunday).

"Father, guide us, as you guide creation according to your law of love. May we love one another and come to perfection in the eternal life prepared for us" (Opening Prayer, 25th Sunday).

"Father, your love for us surpasses all our hopes and desires. Forgive our failings, keep us in your peace and lead us in the way of salvation" (Opening Prayer, 27th Sunday).

"Almighty and ever-living God, our source of power and inspiration, give us strength and joy in serving you as followers of Christ" (Opening Prayer, 29th Sunday).

"God of power and mercy, protect us from all harm. Give us freedom of spirit and health in mind and body to do your work on earth" (Opening Prayer, 32nd Sunday).

"Almighty and merciful God, you break the power of evil and make all things new in your Son Jesus Christ, the King of the universe. May all in heaven and earth acclaim your glory and never cease to praise you" (Opening Prayer, Christ, the King).

The Breviary: The Church's Book Of Daily Praise Of God

The Latin word 'brevis' means a pause or short break in activity. The breviary fills those breaks with praise of God. These words of praise come both from the scriptures and from the writings of holy men and women throughout the ages. The church has made use of modern as well as ancient authors, known and unknown poets of worth, to help us remember the goodness and greatness of God and our complete dependence on him.

When they rise, then at noon, at sunset and before they sleep, the church requires all her priests to pause and recite the praises of God, which reflect the whole liturgical year of salvation. A selection from the four-week cycle of prayers is offered here for the appreciation of their divine images. Like those of the Mass, they are meant to be

155

reflected upon one at a time. Each is masterpiece in its own right.

WEEK I

"Lord, you are the fullness of life, of holiness and of joy. Fill our days and nights with the love of your wisdom, that we may bear fruit in the beauty of holiness, like a tree watered by running streams" (Psalm Prayer 1, Week I, Sunday Readings).

"Lord God, you gave the peoples of the world as the inheritance of your only Son. You crowned him as King of Zion, your holy city, and gave him your church to be his Bride. As he proclaims the law of your eternal kingdom, may we serve him faithfully and so share his royal power forever" (Psalm Prayer 2, Week I, Sunday Readings).

"Lord God, you have given us the great day of rejoicing: Jesus Christ. The stone rejected by the builders has become the cornerstone of the church, our spiritual home. Shed upon your church the rays of your glory, that it may be seen as the gate of salvation open to all nations. Let cries of joy and exultation ring out from its tents, to celebrate the wonder of Christ's resurrection" (Psalm Prayer, Week I, Sunday Daytime).

"Make our lives blameless, Lord. Help us to do what is right and speak what is true, that we may dwell in your tent and find rest on your holy mountain" (Psalm Prayer, Week I, Monday Evening).

"Lord, God, our strength and salvation, put in us the flame of your love and make our love for you grow to a perfect love which reaches to our neighbor" (Psalm Prayer, Week I, Wednesday Readings).

WEEK II

"Let your Word, Father, be a lamp for our feet and a light to our path, so that we may understand what you wish to teach us and follow the

156

path your light marks out for us" (Psalm Prayer, Week 2, Sunday Evening).

"Lord God, eternal shepherd, you so tend the vineyard you planted that now it extends its branches even to the farthest coasts. Look down on your church and come to us. Help us remain in your Son as branches on the vine, that planted firmly in your love, we may testify to the whole world to your great power working everywhere" (Psalm Prayer, Week 2, Thursday Morning).

"Lord, teach us goodness, discipline and wisdom, and these gifts will keep us from becoming hardened by evil, weakened by laziness or ignorant because of foolishness" (Psalm Prayer, Week 2, Thursday Daytime).

"Lord Jesus Christ, you have prepared a quiet place for us in your Father's eternal home. Watch over our welfare on this perilous journey, shade us from the burning heat of day, and keep our lives free of evil until the end" (Psalm Prayer 2, Week 2, Friday Evening).

WEEK III

"Lord, God of the living, you give us lasting youth through the waters of rebirth and happiness through the bread of life. Do not desert us when we are old but help us to follow your will in both good times and bad, so that we may forever praise your faithfulness" (Psalm Prayer, Week 3, Monday Evening).

"Lord Jesus Christ, shepherd of your church, in order to strengthen our faith and to lead us to the kingdom, you renewed and far surpassed the marvels of the old law. Through the uncertainties of this earthly journey, lead us home to the everlasting pastures" (Psalm Prayer 2, Week 3, Thursday Daytime).

WEEK IV

"Lord God, you are the eternal light which illumines the hearts of good people. Help us to love you, to rejoice in your glory and so to live in this world as to avoid harsh judgment in the next. May we come to see the light of your countenance" (Psalm Prayer 2, Week 4, Sunday Evening Prayer II).

"You declared peacemakers happy, Lord Jesus, since they will be called sons of God. Give us that peace which the world cannot give so that your church may be freed from the schemes of arrogant men and, devoted to works of peace, go forward joyfully to meet you, the King of Peace" (Psalm Prayer 3, Week 4, Monday Daytime).

"You have compassion for the sinner, Lord, as a father has compassion for his children. Heal the weakness of your people and save us from lasting death that we may praise and glorify you forever" (Psalm Prayer, Week 4, Wednesday Readings).

"When you took on flesh, Lord Jesus, you made a marriage of mankind with God. Help us to be faithful to your word and endure our exile bravely, until we are called to the heavenly marriage feast, to which the Virgin Mary, exemplar of your church, has preceded us" (Psalm Prayer 2, Week 4, Saturday Daytime).

CHAPTER FIFTEEN

GETTING TO KNOW THE TRUE GOD

God has chosen to reveal himself to me through many different people. Some of these people, I'm convinced, knew him well. Others, however never seemed to have established any deep personal relationship with him. So, like most folks, I've had to deal with a mixture of correct and incorrect, or shall I say true and faulty ideas about God.

I don't recall my parents as overly pious people. They were good, ordinary folks who struggled to live and who asked the "Good God" for help in their struggles. I honestly don't recall my parents' having taught me anything specific about God except that he loved me and would help me if I asked him. They sent me and my sisters to a Catholic school, ensuring that we went to church and received the sacraments. My parents also showed pleasure when we learned our prayers and hymns and passed our religious exams. They also celebrated our first reception of the sacraments and saw to it that we continued to receive them on a regular basis. My parents never tolerated bad language, selfishness, disobedience, discourteous behavior, fighting, stealing, lying, or any semblance of sexual misconduct. Our mistakes in these matters were usually punished swiftly, but we were not harped on.

When I look back on things, it seems that I came to know God as some great unseen benefactor or protector whom we acknowledged on Sunday, before and after a meal or at bedtime. He was always present. He was someone we could call on to help us survive our difficulties. It isn't easy for me to analyze those distant times, but in attempt I would say that I picked up a sense that:

- God, like Mom and Dad, was good and wanted us to be good.
- He knew us personally and kept an eye on us.
- God was interested in us, especially in our behavior.
- He would help us, if we asked him perseveringly in prayer.

- He would forgive us, if we were sorry and acknowledged our wrongs.
- He would also punish us, if we didn't repent, because he didn't want us to spoil our lives, or the lives of others.

This contribution of my simple-living, hard-working parents, I have come to realize, has been of inestimable value to me, truly irreplaceable.

Our teachers, the Missionary Sisters of the Most Sacred Heart of Jesus, seemed to have influenced me more than anyone. A few of the Sisters were strict disciplinarians; most of them were extremely patient and kind women who took a personal interest in each one of us. They taught us that we were all God's children, that God loved to listen to our prayers and songs, that he wanted us to be good like he is, that if we asked him he would help us, and that God would forgive us when we made mistakes, if we were sorry. They introduced us to Bible stories and to stories of holy men and women who loved God. The Sisters taught us to memorize answers to questions about God, about the world, human beings, about Jesus and his teachings concerning life, death and the after-life, about the wonderful community or church that Jesus founded in order to help us live good lives.

In retrospect, the priests of our parish and those who later taught me in high school did not teach me anything fundamentally new. At best they seem to have complemented the religious formation of my parents and the Sisters, occasionally adding some new insight or deepening my convictions about God and what he wanted us to do. Sometimes special preachers, however, who were invited to the parish seemed to have influenced me and others to some extent also, for I recall lining up with a great number of people outside the confessionals at the end of their talks.

The desire to be good, but also the fear of going to hell, seemed to dominate the thoughts of people when I was young. Yes, God was good and would forgive our failings no matter how often we committed them, but if we died unrepentant of some serious sin, we would wind up in hell. And there were lots and lots of ways to commit serious sins. The catechisms of those times dealt greatly with personal sins, especially those of commission. Unwittingly, I believe, this led us to develop a very stern image of God. It seems, too, that Catholics of the time stressed avoiding evil rather than doing good; we concentrated on stopping evil-doers rather than encouraging those who promoted justice. Perhaps this is basically why so few Catholics before the 'sixties initiated movements to tackle the problems of racial and social injustice in the U.S. and around the world. To be sure, we cooperated with leaders who solicited our help, but we found it hard to break out of this pattern of teaching, which dwelt more on our personal welfare and salvation than on involvement in the City of Man.

We also had everything neatly worked out in black-and-white categories: good and bad, right and wrong. Our priests and catechisms had all the answers for how we should live. All we had to do was follow them in order to be happy and at peace.

I liked the feeling of belonging to a church that had all the answers on every issue of good and evil. Unconsciously there developed in me a desire to be associated with the leaders of this church. I believe the desire to become a priest arose when I was about ten or eleven years old. Consequently, toward the end of my final year in grade school I asked my parents for permission to study for the priesthood in a high school seminary run by the Missionaries of the Sacred Heart. They thought I was too young to leave the nest, so permission was denied. So I entered Northeast Catholic High School for Boys in Philadelphia and did my studies there.

My high school teachers, the Oblates of St. Francis DeSales were all no-nonsense people, and those who taught us religion carried on the tradition of having all the answers to any doctrinal or moral question. We were told over and over that the Catholic Church was the only

161

true Christian church; salvation was attained by belonging to this church and by following her teachings; the Pope, bishops and priests of the Catholic church were the teachers par excellence. Thus my old desire to be associated with them was reinforced. I wanted to become one of these elite teachers. I wanted to bring the answers of the church to people still living in the "darkness" of sin.

However, desiring to do something and actually attempting it are two different things. I graduated from high school and drifted off to work in one of the local factories, without making a decision regarding studies for the priesthood. In fact, I held two jobs: a full-time job in a factory and a part-time job in a local grocery store. Work, sports and evenings out with friends kept me quite distracted. Then one day after work I received an invitation to visit a missionary who was staying with our pastor. The Sisters had never forgotten that I had once expressed a desire to become a missionary. They thought I might profit from meeting this man.

I thus set out on a new course of my journey in search of the true God. The visitor, Fr. Janssen, asked a few questions and listened to my story of aspiration for the priesthood. With compelling logic he said, "If you don't enter and try, you'll never know whether or not God intends you to become one of his priests." He then handed me some application forms. I took them home and told my parents that I had decided to enter the training program of the Missionaries of the Sacred Heart. My parents listened, seemed happy and said they would pray for me. That was in late spring of 1950. By fall I began my studies.

The first part of the program called for at least one year of intensive Latin studies. I was told that the textbooks in the major seminary were written in the ancient language; so all students for the priesthood had to master it. I struggled through the assignments, passed the exams and then applied for the novitiate, known as the "spiritual" year of formation. The novitiate was designed to introduce a candidate to religious life as lived by the Missionaries of the Sacred

Heart. The congregation had been founded in 1854 in France to help people around the world to experience God as the God of Love. The history of the Society had shown that people needed this experience and welcomed it not only in France, but also around the globe. The program naturally included formal classroom instructions, but also provided us a variety of tasks designed to test the generosity, flexibility, self-control and perseverance of the candidates.

Our director, as regular as a clock in his instructions, but as unpredictable in mood as the weather, communicated his great love of God, church and congregation to us. Like a drill-sergeant in the marines, however he left us in doubt as to whether any of us were fit to be admitted to the ranks. After all, the professed members would carry on the great traditions of preaching and service around the world.

As the eldest of our group of eight, I was entrusted with the task of scheduling jobs and making sure things were in order. If anything went wrong (and occasionally it did) the director blasted me, but didn't needle me about it afterwards. Only many years later did I come to realize what he really thought of me. My mother showed me an extremely tender letter which he had written to her and dad almost 35 years ago, in which he praised my parents for my early formation and expressed high hopes that I would prove to be a worthy Missionary of the Sacred Heart.

During the novitiate I began to appreciate the great God of Love and how he had manifested his love for me and all people. I also began to realize that most people did not view God as a loving Trio of Persons. This realization would be reinforced when I left the sheltered world of the novitiate, and entered major seminary, where I carried out my philosophical, theological and scriptural studies. For many people, God was some impersonal force who set the world in motion, and then abdicated its control to people. For others he was a super-cop keeping an eye on the moral doings of mortals, threatening the rebellious with dire punishments both in this world and the next.

Others saw him as some giant unseen benefactor who could be manipulated with prayers and religious practices.

Almost all of these people thought of God only in relationship to themselves and to their own aspirations. They never developed a genuine personal relationship with him. God was not someone to be discovered, listened to, talked to in loving dialogue, worshiped in service of the neglected and poor. Rather he was ignored, feared, or viewed as someone who could be coaxed into doing what they wanted him to do. Consequently I discovered many people also had difficulty developing a loving relationship with other human beings. Their attitude toward God affected their relationships with people, most of these they ignored. They looked upon the rich and powerful with envy and fear, manipulating those who had what they wanted, blind in a real sense to all but themselves.

It seemed to me, most people never break out of the centrifugal force of self-interest, and into the freedom which God intends them to have. They don't break out, because they can't break out until God enables them to. And God can't enable them until they get to know him as he really is. They will not get to know him, because they think it is a waste of time to listen and reflect, or to share and to help others without a hidden agenda.

In a sense, none of my philosophical or theological studies prepared me adequately for the massive indifference, unwillingness to change, impatience with new ideas, or religious tokenism which I would face as a priest and missionary. I found that most people just were not hepped up about developing a personal relationship with God. Even some of those who did join prayer groups seemed to be more interested in finding solace than in discovering the God of Love. Many were not prepared to hear him call them to a fresh way of looking at the world.

Saying this does not mean that I fault the training I received in the seminary. I simply did not appreciate the need to develop a deep personal relationship with God as the cornerstone of my life, preaching and work. In a confused way, I suppose I knew this truth. But only now, some forty years later, can I formulate it in words. Only now can I recognize those who seem to have attained this goal. Only now can I say that unless this is achieved, we remain restless, discontented and ineffectual, no matter how successful we seem to be.

St. John, in his first letter, came to the heart of this matter when he said: "God's love for us was revealed when he sent into the world his only Son, so that we could have life through him. This is the love I mean: not our love for God, but God's love for us when he sent his Son to be the sacrifice that takes our sins away. My dear people, since God has loved us so much, we too should love one another" *(1 Jn 4:9-11)*.

We begin to develop a personal relationship with God when we examine what God has done for us, what he has said to us, what he asks of us. We begin by admitting that we don't know him, but want to. We begin by comparing the ideas we have about him with those he now reveals to us. We begin by listening and reflecting on what he has said and done in our lives and the lives of others.

This seems easy, but almost no one wants to do it on a daily basis. Why? I believe the answer lies in a lack of conviction that this is the most important goal to be achieved in life. Most people are not really convinced that spending time listening to God will help them to be truly human, that he will improve their outlook on the world, on themselves and other people, on their jobs and human situations. Most are comfortable with their current outlooks and don't want God to rock their boat. They excuse themselves on the basis of being too busy. The demands of life leave no room for the luxury of quiet listening, reflecting and sharing. So nothing really changes for the better. The indifferent remain indifferent. The fearful remain fearful. The self-righteous remain self-righteous. The self-satisfied remain self-satisfied.

Lest these words seem arrogant, I want you to know that it took me a long time to develop this conviction. I should have developed it sooner, because the training I received in the novitiate and major seminary emphasized the importance of spending at least an hour each day in reflective reading of the Sacred Scriptures and other holy writings to nourish personal union with Christ. However, once I left the organized schedule of the training centers and plunged into ministry, I found it easy to excuse myself from the daily practice. Everything else seemed to be more important:

- I needed the extra sleep.
- People were waiting to see me.
- I had visiting to do.
- I had to prepare a talk or lesson.
- Reports were due.
- I needed to do shopping, or repair something.
- It was too hot; I couldn't concentrate; I was too tired and needed to relax with light reading, T.V., etc.

As a result I gradually became a competent pastor, teacher, preacher, builder, administrator who ran a good show. This same pastor wondered in his quieter moments if anybody was really absorbing the Good News he had come to bring. Sure, people were coming to Mass and sending their kids for instructions in the faith. Sure, they were coming to the sacraments and cooperating on church projects. But unchristian attitudes and practices still flourished in the same people. What I failed to realize was that I could not affect any fundamental and lasting change in the people I served. Why? Because they had not developed a deep personal relationship with Christ. They had not developed it because they understood religion in terms of answers to questions, things required to be done on certain days or at certain times to remain part of the community, rites to be celebrated to ward off dangers or to bring blessings, laws to be obeyed so that punishments could be avoided.

Unwittingly I nourished this understanding of religion by my outlook on my role. I was the ordained, commissioned, professional religious

166

leader of the catholic community, rather than a friend of Jesus, who wanted other people to know how he had affected my life for the better, how he could also affect theirs. So I was content when the kids knew the answers to my questions, when the church was packed and people listened, when they came to help with church projects, when our institutions were running smoothly and our personnel were happy.

What I couldn't comprehend was why magical or pagan practices never faded away in the villages or towns; *why* migrants stopped going to church when they moved to new areas; *why* students who attended the universities frequently gave up their faith; *why* catholic politicians were indistinguishable from those with anti-Christian views; *why* those who joined the public service institutions upheld anti-Christian practices; *why* married people found it so hard to be faithful to each other; *why* so few Catholics had any impact on the social or political order of things.

It has taken me a long time to discover what I should have known from the start: you can't give what you haven't got. I didn't have the unshakeable conviction that I had to spend time daily listening and reflecting on what God and Christ were saying to me. So I could not communicate this conviction to the people I served. I did not make top priority my development of a deep personal relationship with Jesus, so I couldn't inspire others to do it, either.

This does not mean that I had ceased thinking of God, or about religious matters. I thought about them often, but not in personal dialogue with Christ. I considered it important to communicate the truths of our faith, to celebrate Mass and the sacraments, to manage carefully the finance and records of the parish or institute, to oversee the construction of schools, churches, dispensaries, houses for personnel, to visit people and help them with a hundred-and-one favors.

What I overlooked was the great truth that only God through his Son and Spirit effects fundamental changes in people. To the degree that we open ourselves to him, to that degree he brings about these changes. We're like clams with all kinds of nutrients swirling around them, but who aren't nourished until they open their shells and take the food in. The teachings of God, the life of Christ, the working of the Spirit in the lives of holy men and women, are like so many swirling spiritual nutrients. They affect little or nothing until each person takes them into regularly his mind and heart. Learning answers to questions, attending church on Sunday, receiving the sacraments have their role to play in our development, but they can never replace the effort involved in daily listening to God and reflecting on what he says to us through the scriptures, and through the persons and events of our lives.

Daily heart-to-heart communication with God establishes a genuine bond of love that drives out fear, gives strength to our wills, calm to our hearts, clarity to our minds and inspiration to our beings. This communication drives out fear of punishment for past sins and of future failure, because it reveals the loving forgiveness and power of God. It focuses our attention on God and not on ourselves. The words of Micah suddenly become so vivid: "What god can compare with you: taking fault away, pardoning crime, not cherishing anger for ever, but delighting in showing mercy. Once more have pity on us, tread down our faults; throw away all our sins to the bottom of the sea" (Mi 7:18-19).

While not eliminating the need for a wise spiritual director with whom we can share our insights and aspirations so as to keep our balance, this daily openness to God is so fundamental to growth that nothing can replace it. In the providence of God each one of us is called to grow through both communal and private worship. Each has its place. Neither can replace the other.

Communal worship, for example, makes us aware of our solidarity with God and with one another. It keeps the great themes of salvation before us. It makes us aware of the whole of Scripture, the great traditions of the church, the prayers, songs and actions that help us know and celebrate God's goodness. It gives us Christ's strength in sacraments that help us to live our lives with and for God.

Private worship allows us to savor and absorb what we have participated in and heard, saving us from passivity. Thus personal worshiping permits us to work out the personal implications of what we have celebrated, allowing God to expand and deepen the knowledge we have acquired. It fans our love for God and people. It allows us to express ourselves creatively, without worrying about the feelings of others.

The Gospels reveal that Jesus worshiped in the temple with the people of his community. They tell us also that he spent a great deal of time in private prayer. During these very sessions he derived the insights and strength to carry out his mission.

Christ encouraged his followers to pray not only together, but also in secret. "When you pray, go to your private room and, when you have shut your door, pray to your Father who is in that secret place, and your Father who sees all that is done in secret will reward you" *(Mt 6:6)*. The reward is first an increase of faith in, and sensitivity to, the goodness of God, who loves you, and everything he has made.

The deeper our conviction of God's love, the more liberated we become from personal sin and from worry over past sins. This, I believe, is ultimately why God entered human affairs: to liberate us from sin that we might rejoice in his goodness and power. This becomes abundantly clear as we reflect on the Old and New Testaments and on God's action in our own lives. As the Book of Wisdom says: "You love all that exists and abhor nothing of what you have made, for had you hated anything, you would not have formed it. And how, had you not willed it, could a thing persist, how be conserved, if not called forth by you? You spare all things because all things are yours, Lord, lover of life, you whose imperishable spirit is in all. Little by little, therefore, you correct

169

those who offend, you admonish and remind them of how they have sinned, so that they may abstain from evil and trust in you, Lord" *(Wis 11:25 ff. & 12:1-2)*.

After a period of time, people who persevere in private prayer find themselves speaking less and listening more. They expect God to reveal himself through the Scriptures, through reflection upon people and events and he does not disappoint them. Gradually they lose their compulsion to leap-frog from event to event or to read hurriedly, content to dwell on short passages. They linger over phrases, even words that reveal God's tenderness. Their words of praise become less elaborate, but are uttered with intense sincerity.

They come away from their secret place, reluctantly and are eager to return to it. For they know, like Peter on Tabor, that "it is wonderful for us to be here" *(Mt 17:4)*.

I have often wondered where the great saints got such energy, calm and courage, and now it is crystal clear these traits arose from their private sessions with the Lord. Like Paul they could say with complete honesty: "I know how to be poor and I know how to be rich, too. I have been through my initiation and now I am ready for anything anywhere: full stomach or empty stomach, poverty or plenty. There is nothing I cannot master with the help of the One who gives me strength" *(Phil 4:12-14)*.

Mother Teresa has told us repeatedly that more people are starving for love than for bodily food, and that loneliness is more crippling than disease. But the good news is that regular private sessions of quiet prayer remove these feelings. In them God becomes real, a loving friend who listens and speaks, who gives insights, wisdom, strength and courage. Loneliness and the feeling of abandonment disappear forever. Union with God gradually becomes more important than personal health, fame, fortune or friends. Maintaining this union through personal daily prayer becomes a must, an item of top priority. Isaiah's admonition of God to Israel is taken to heart:

"Your salvation lies in conversion and tranquility, your strength in complete trust" *(Is 30:15)*.

To help people believe in the goodness of God and turn to him in daily, regular sessions of private prayer has become an important goal of my life. I believe that this is one of the greatest things I can do for others. There is nothing better that will help them to achieve openness of mind, peace of heart and willingness to share with those less fortunate. There is nothing better that will foster appreciation of the church, the Mass, the sacraments, the Scriptures, and the lives of holy men and women... all in God's good time and in accord with each person's personal history and capacity.

Another of my goals is to help people understand and use the Sacred Scriptures to nourish their daily private prayer. The Bible is unique among all books, for through the sacred texts God reveals himself, while unfolding our marvelous dignity and destiny. Through them he clarifies for us things that hurt or further our relationship with him and others. Through them he affirms his undying love for each one of us.

The Scriptural messages of God are timeless, living and personal, although they were written by human beings who have long since died. Once we appreciate this truth, these loving words bear careful reading and re-reading, for each passage communicates directly from a God who loves us more than we will ever be able to comprehend.

CHAPTER SIXTEEN

PERSEVERANCE IN PRAYER

Hope, in the Scriptures, is inextricably bound up with patient waiting, with perseverance: "Be patient, brothers, until the Lord's coming" (Jas 5:7). "Charity is patient" (1 Cor 13:4). "Do not be impatient in prayer" (Sir 7:10). "Better patience than pride" (Eccl 7:9). There are literally hundreds of texts like these which reinforce the need to "hang in there" until the Lord chooses to reveal himself and reward our longings for insight and consolation.

Patient waiting is not something we human beings endure gracefully. It is not a virtue that we inherit, or that we imbibe with our mother's milk. It is an acquired virtue, acquired by those with strong beliefs and desires.

We know from personal experience, and from the experiences of others, that expertise in any matter is acquired from persevering study and from many long hours of practice. Arturo Rubinstein said that he spent an average of fourteen hours a day at the piano. For years, Lee Trevino hit at least 1,000 golf balls a day to perfect his swing. Yet somehow or other, we, who yearn to know more about God, find ourselves reluctant to spend any notable amount of time listening to God.

God always respects our freedom. He does not force himself into our lives. He waits for us to invite him to reveal himself. He is not slow to do this, although it may seem to us that at times he is. However, we are the ones who are not tuned in; we are the ones that are not calmed down; we are the ones with the blurred vision. Our agitated minds, our wayward hearts, our undisciplined wills, all prevent us from absorbing the stream of divine revelations which flow unceasingly from our loving God.

All the saints, and all spiritual writers of merit, have recognized this

172

truth. They know that God is always revealing himself. So they work at perfecting their ability to listen through prayer. And the more they listen, the more they receive. The more they receive, the more fascinated they become. The more fascinated they become, the more they want to listen and receive. They more they receive, they more they want to share. The more they share, the more they receive.

Dom Chautard, in his classic work *The Soul of the Apostolate*, reflects on the paradox of prayer. He says that those who claim they can't find the time in which to pray will wonder, if they make time for this important matter, how they ever lived without it. They will discover, like the great saints, even new physical energy from it, for there is an intimate connection between our spirit and body.

"The immense labors accomplished, in spite of precarious health, by a St. Augustine, a St. John Chrysostom, a St. Bernard, a St. Thomas Aquinas, or a St. Vincent de Paul, amaze us. But we are even more astonished to see how these men, in spite of their almost unceasing work, kept themselves in the most constant union with God. Quenching, more than others, their thirst at the source of life, by contemplation, these saints drew from it the most unlimited capacity for work" (*The Soul of the Apostolate*, Part One, Number Five).

Those who want to satisfy their unspoken yearning to see God must, first of all, decide on a daily, sizeable amount of time in which to listen to God and reflect on his revelations. Experienced spiritual directors believe that this must be, minimally, half an hour. Why? It takes time to calm down, to relax, to concentrate--perhaps as much as five minutes. It also takes time to read slowly, thoughtfully. It takes time to reflect, to ask questions of the Lord, to express feelings, to savor what has been understood and appreciated. God is eternal, but we creatures are time bound: men and women whose minds and feelings, just like our bodies, need time to warm up, so that we can respond.

These same spiritual directors advise adherence to this regimen, and reluctance to extend the time to an hour, unless a person is determined to persevere in the new time frame. They advise against shortening the time, except for the most serious reasons. Our old adversary understands what the Lord can do for us and through us. So he will work on our impatience, anxiety level, need to do things, and much more, to get us to shorten the time or excuse ourselves for a hundred-and-one good reasons.

Those who are experienced in the art of prayer advise us to begin by sitting in a relaxed way, unhampered by any books or papers. They encourage us to take in and exhale a dozen deep breaths while saying a simple phrase like: "Come, Lord Jesus" or "Come, Holy Spirit." This simple exercise quiets the mind and emotions and prepares a person for attention to what will be read or heard or recalled.

They also advise us to stop and react to whatever strikes us, to express our delight, our gratitude, our amazement, our confusion, our desire ... whatever! We are encouraged to let these feelings wash over our soul, bringing it peace, delight, new strength, before moving on. We are warned not to be in a hurry to move on, but to stay with our insight, our feelings until we find ourselves drifting into distractions. One single insight into one single truth can change a person's entire life!

Daily prayer of this nature will develop within us the unshakeable conviction that the wonderful God who made and sustains all things truly loves us and all people. We will begin to feel comfortable in his presence and delight in discovering manifestations of his goodness and power. This sense of wonder and profound worth will sustain us in times of difficulty and influence our outlook on those with whom we live and work. We will feel different--more joyful and at peace--and even notice a difference in our energy level.

Others, too, will begin to notice the change in us. They may be encouraged to ask us what has made the difference in our life. This will be our opportunity to share our story, our search to see the face of God.

174

EPILOGUE

"O Lord, your truth reaches even to the clouds. The clouds pass, but heaven remains.

"The preachers of your word pass from this life to the next, but your Scripture is stretched over the peoples until the end of time....

"The scroll shall be folded, and the grass over which it was spread shall pass with its glory, but your word endures forever.

"Now we see in the darkness of clouds and in the mirror of heaven, and not as it is: because though we are now beloved by your Son, it has not yet appeared what we shall be.

"He has seen us through the lattice of flesh and has caressed us and inflamed us, and we run after the odor of his ointments.

"But when he shall appear, we shall be like him, because we shall see him as he is.

"It will be ours, O Lord, to see him as he is, but it is not for us yet."

(*The Confessions of St. Augustine*, Book Thirteen, XV)

175

INDEX

176

177

178